About the author

Malcolm 'Blocker' Johnson was born in East Twerton in Bath but moved at a tender age to Odd Down on the southern side of the city. He attended St. Luke's Primary School from where he gained a scholarship to King Edward's School in Bath.

From 1964 to 1969 he studied at Durham University where he gained a First in French and German, wrote a thesis on the novels of Emile Zola and played cricket for the University. He taught French and German between 1969 and 1979 at Richard Taunton College in Southampton and was Head of Modern Languages at Dauntsey's School in West Lavington near Devizes until retirement in 2005.

From his earliest years Malcolm was a member of Hampset Cricket Club in Bath. He played for the club from 1960 until 2006.

His playing record reads as follows:

Batting:
Innings 451, Not out 200, Total Runs 1,667, Average 6.64.
Bowling:
Overs 10,508.3, Maidens 1,692, Runs 35,060, Wickets 2,181, Average 16.08.
Fielding:
Catches 176.

WATCH OUT !
'ERE COMES BURFY

MALCOLM 'BLOCKER' JOHNSON

CHARLCOMBE BOOKS

Charlcombe Books
17 George's Road, Bath BA1 6EY
Tel 01225-335813

First published 2011

ISBN 978 0 9568510 2 4

Printed and bound in Great Britain by
Midway Colour Print, Trowbridge, Wiltshire

CONTENTS

Hampset Cricket Club from the air, hemmed in on three sides
by the houses of Somerdale Avenue, Bloomfield Rise and Bloomfield Drive
(photograph taken in 1997 by Andy Perryman)

Preface

This book is written in homage to Hampset Cricket Club. Small, unpretentious, unassuming, welcoming, hidden, so many adjectives could be used to describe you. The last one, 'hidden', is perhaps surprising but, set as you are amongst a series of streets and ordinary, fairly nondescript houses, there are many who have lived near you for years without knowing of your existence. Time and again over the years opposition players have reported asking people for directions to Hampset when just a few yards away, only to be met with a blank stare. I see that they have now put up a special sign to you in Rush Hill in an attempt to help those lost. Sat-navs perhaps do the same but hidden away you remain.

Although it is now over forty years since I lived within a cricket ball's throw of your 'Tiny' Morris-built clubhouse, your Mike Ball-mown outfield and your Perryman-and-generations-of-members-carefully-tended wickets, you remain a home from home, a familiar haven of tranquillity. The years took me away from you in geographical terms, to Durham, to France, back to Durham, to Southampton and finally back, a little nearer, to West Lavington, but I was never able to play anywhere else.

I drove miles in a series of motors, Minis, Maxis, Maestros and others to play at Bloomfield Rise and sundry grounds on the Hampset circuit; to have performed elsewhere would have seemed unfaithful and adulterous and so to you I owe forty six playing years of happy wedded bliss.

Just before I finally hung up my boots at a party for my sixtieth birthday I was presented with a book by Hampset member Adrian 'Woden' Jeffrey, so-called because of his Viking-like appearance and demeanour and not, I trust, for any propensity for raping and pillaging. This book *66 n.o. Tales of a Village Cricketer* by Roger Northam, which consisted of a series of memories of playing for Hambrook, Stapleton and the Willows, all teams from the Bristol area, was fascinating and entertaining, for the first two of these clubs had always been on our fixture list and there was even a chapter on Hampset within it. Whilst reading Roger's reminiscences it occurred to me that something similar should be done for Hampset and so I started, stopped for a long time, picked up a pen again and finally produced this modest tome.

My second hero is Odd Down, the area of Bath in which Hampset C.C lies concealed from the world rushing by. All the Japanese, American, European and other visitors who come to marvel at the Roman Baths and the elegant architecture in the World Heritage City of my birth are unlikely to take you in, this oddly named, ordinary, not-worth-a-second-glance outlying district of the city they come fleetingly to see.

Not much has changed since my childhood and youth; like everywhere else you have lost a few shops, pubs and petrol stations, throttled out of existence by the emergence of the all-powerful supermarket. Noad's Corner is again in need of the revamp it has always seemed to have required. Sources of local employment such as Clark's have gone and people of a number of different nationalities have arrived to join your unremarkable population, but you are essentially the same as in the days when we as children used to roam your streets and pathways.

You were never particularly fashionable. Beau Nash and his cronies never considered building their elegant structures in your midst, preferring to look across to you, no doubt with a certain air of disdain, from their south-facing mansions on the opposite hills. Way, way back Bladud and his diseased swine are said to have descended from the hills into the boggy marshes of what was to become one of Europe's greatest spas, Bath Spa, this is Bath Spa, as the station announcer constantly reminds us, and accidentally discovered the healing properties of the local hot waters. Exactly whence they came has not, I think, been recorded but I would not mind betting that it was from Odd Down's shivering slopes that they came down to roll themselves in the mud and become miraculously cured.

When I gave my address to people who did not know Bath at all, they often assumed that I had inadvertently written the first d instead of an l, for who could willingly name their area as odd? But Odd you were and have remained though my memories of you belie your name for odd you were not. You were just home to me and a whole generation of youngsters who were to become some of the best club cricketers in the area.

This was never intended to be a history of Hampset Cricket Club, that has already been expertly done by Alan Hack, middle of the trio of Odd Down born Hacks who figured with distinction in Hampset scorebooks over a long period, in his book *Sting in the Tail – Fifty Years of Hampset Cricket*. This present book set out to be a series of cricketing reminiscences à la Roger Northam but it seems to have turned into a more general chronicle of growing up. Since I grew up at and with Hampset Cricket Club perhaps this is not surprising, but my two heroes remain an unsung cricket club and its equally unsung surroundings. I have not checked the veracity of any of the facts, nor sought to embroider any of the memories. Almost certainly there are errors but I hope I may be forgiven for making them.

Opening the innings

My introduction to Hampset was not an auspicious one. It came about as the result of one of two momentous announcements by 'Oggy Woggy Goggy', when I was about six years old. 'Oggy Woggy Goggy' was the somewhat irreverent title given by pupils to the Headmaster of the then St Luke's, now St Philip's, Primary School, Odd Down. His real name was Mr H.W.G. Smart and his wife Mrs Smart was in charge of the first class, what would now be more clinically called 'Reception' and whose sole aim in life seemed to be to put children to sleep at lunch-time. No pupils, of course, ever became privy to what the Headmaster's resplendent initials actually stood for, hence the resonant, rhyming soubriquet which I could rarely bring myself to use, perhaps as it rang like a rather insulting reaction to all of us who, like my brother Master C.A.F. Johnson and I, had three forenames. There was no secret behind mine. Malcolm was after my father's war-time Commanding Officer, apparently a member of the tobacco-producing Player family, surely the reason why my father, as a post-pay-day Friday treat, smoked Player's Navy Cut over the weekend but reverted to the cheaper Woodbines later. This Player had emerged unscathed from the activities in North Africa but had perished as they made their way up through Italy, a true hero to us, particularly as his eponymous family firm produced the best cigarette cards, the most valuable when doing 'swops'. Then a bit more prosaically came Kenneth, my father's first name and Frederick, that of my uncle.

Master CAF Johnson and Master MKF Johnson,
captured for posterity at Mower's Studio, Bath.

One day Mr H.W.G. Smart summoned us all to the hall at a time which was not usually given over to an Assembly. I think in my case it interrupted a particularly tense game of Rounders, the closest we usually got to cricket, in which, as ever, no doubt, the soppy girls were complaining that the boys threw the ball too hard and fast. The only girl who was able to cope was the redoubtable Theresa Smith who, because she regularly managed to swat away a series of beamers, was the only girl worthy of any attention throughout my Primary School career. Her later cruel rejection of me as a country dancing partner put me off the opposite sex for a few years and off dancing for ever.

From the field / playground we trooped into the Hall, the boys of our class in daps, shirts and shorts, held up by the classic expanding belt secured by a silver, snake-shaped buckle, the girls with their dresses still tucked into their blue knickers. Mr H.W.G. Smart solemnly announced that the King was dead and that he would be succeeded by the young Princess Elizabeth. I remember wondering at the time about the use of the word 'succeed', what would this youthful lady have to try to manage to do exactly? This first pronouncement by Mr H.W.G. Smart did not have much immediate effect on us, although a little later on we did get a Coronation mug and a whole school visit to see *The Conquest of Everest* at the Odeon in town. I knew already from the Magic Robot, a quirky forerunner of Trivial Pursuits, which one of us had received for Christmas, that Everest was the highest mountain in the world and now it came to life in full colour on the big screen. At the beginning of this epic there was spectacular scenery with a string of men laden with backpacks, some of whom were more laden than others, who endlessly crossed wobbly bridges over torrents of icy waters. Later on the cast dwindled to just two men, one tall, one short, wearing goggles like those who rode around on and in motor cycles and sidecars, and whose grizzled beards became increasingly covered in ice which looked most uncomfortable. Sherpa Tenzing and Edmund Hillary, as yet without his 'Sir' which Mr Tenzing to my knowledge never acquired, going through life known simply as Sherpa, inched their way to the top with the help of little pickaxes and boots with spikes in longer even than those which were nailed into football boots and there they took a few photos and triumphantly planted a flag – a Union Jack, of course. They made their way back down much quicker than they had gone up and were greeted by their leader Sir John Hunt with a lot of smiling, grinning and back slapping. We'd recently won the war and now we'd conquered Everest. The young queen had a lot to live up to.

Mr H.W.G. Smart's second pronouncement was to have a greater, long-term effect, on me at least. It was delivered at a slightly later, scheduled assembly amongst a lot of other routine material in a tone of less solemnity than the news of the king's demise and the succession of the new queen. He announced that the local cricket club, Hampset Cricket Club, which was to be found at the other end of Bloomfield Rise, would be running coaching classes for boys (none of this equality nonsense then) on Tuesday evenings at 6.30 pm. We had become vaguely aware of the existence of this establishment from our bike rides in our surrounding area. Along Bloomfield Road, past Shellard's Tower, over the brow of the hill, left into Bloomfield Drive just before

Bloomfield Crescent, along the Drive, up Somerdale Avenue and back home became one of our many itineraries as we radiated further and further from the prefabs. One day, however, someone turned left off the Drive and along an unnamed, unmade-up road which ran along the back of the houses and it was here on the left that we first became aware of the small patch of land which was obviously some sort of sports ground. A bit later on we must have taken this route on a Saturday or a Sunday afternoon or perhaps on a day when a mid-week fixture was being played. On this occasion we found the area peopled by white-flannelled cricketers and all of them were in white, not just a few, as happened in matches up the Players (Odd Down Playing Fields) with the others wearing ordinary trousers held up by a stout belt, perhaps a white shirt and an off-white pair of daps. No, here they were all in white; a couple even wore fetching cravats in dark blue and light blue club colours. This was obviously much more serious, and we gazed with much respectful interest from outside the boundary fence, not daring to go in to take a closer look.

It was to this semi-familiar place of evidently serious cricket that we – my brother Chris, Brian Buck, a few other boys from our estate and I, all led by my mother – repaired on the appointed Tuesday evening, in accordance with Mr H.W.G. Smart's announcement in the assembly. On crossing through the club's front gates, something I would do thousands of times in the future, our eyes met with the sight of several cricketing activities already taking place under the supervision of what were presumably accomplished senior playing members. We were greeted by a slightly more elderly man with whom my mother was already acquainted, Mr Victor 'Rosey' Rosenburg. My brother, Brian Buck and the others, who must all have been about 10 or 11 years old at the time, were quickly sent to join in with a particular group and then attention was brought to bear on me. My mother and this imposing looking Janus went into a bit of a huddle and I could just make out a few snatches of their ominous sounding conversation: 'too young … hard ball … might get hurt … in a year or two.' My mother came sheepishly over to me, no doubt anticipating the reaction of her second-born. "They say you're too young," she explained. "They're afraid you might get hurt playing with a hard ball with lots of older boys. Come back in a couple of years, they said." "A couple of years?" I cried. "Tell them I've always played with the older boys. I've been using a 'ard ball for years," I exclaimed not without a little exaggeration. But this Rosey and some fellow conspirators he had enlisted were adamant. Years before Health and Safety was even a glint in some killjoy's eye, I was to be denied participation for some spuriously cautious reason.

"Come on Malc, we'll go back home and I'll get you some sweets from Sly's on the way," was my mother's pathetic attempt to counter the by now fairly obvious disappointment which was manifesting itself in floods of tears. Off we trudged, me still wailing, back home. Not even the prospect of liquorice, a sherbet dab, four-a-penny fruit salads and black jacks or even a quarter of pineapple rock, all now no longer the subject of rationing, could assuage the tears of frustration at a great cricketing career nipped so heartlessly in the bud.

Victor 'Rosey' Rosenburg, the initially misjudged 'destroyer of childhood dreams'. Here 'Rosey' is pictured in umpire mode either just before or just after a match at Bloomfield Rise. The bell, used for years to summon teams to battle in Hampset's home matches, suggests it was before a game. The refreshment was almost certainly Stone's ginger beer, his favourite tipple.

Lyn Morgan told me recently of a match in Usk that 'Rosey' umpired before the war. Towards the end of the home side's innings a boy of about 12 came in and, although he was not strong enough to hit the ball far, he impressed with some elegant stroke play, ending up about 30 not out. 'Rosey' went to congratulate the boy, who was called Allan Watkins, giving him a red and white glass marble to keep as a memento of his innings and to bring him luck. Many years later when Watkins was an established county and test cricketer he was playing for Glamorgan against Somerset, and 'Rosey' went to the pavilion to speak to him. "Mister Watkins," he said, "you won't remember me but some years ago I umpired a match in which you played and gave you a marble." "I do remember," he said and, going to his cricket bag, produced the spherical talisman. Such interest in youth on Rosey's part was not apparent to me at the time.

Inconsolable I may have been but beaten I was not. When the next Tuesday came round and the 'big' boys were preparing for their second Hampset coaching session, I suggested that I might at least be allowed to watch. In fact I must have proposed such a move countless times since finally my mother gave in. "Alright, I'll take you over and we'll ask them." The same crocodile as the week before wended its way to Bloomfield Rise, to be met by the same destroyer of childhood dreams. More whispered conversations. "I don't see why not, as long as he sits well away from the balls that fly around." Why was this living obstacle to youthful enjoyment so obsessed with the hardness of cricket balls? And so it was that for a few weeks I sat and watched what was going on. A privileged few, who were already quite adept, were creamed off to practise in the nets at the bottom of the ground with a fairly small, dapper man who, when he himself occasionally bowled to illustrate a point to an aspiring batsman, did so with a series of jerky movements reminiscent of the Magic Robot who dispensed us general knowledge indoors on rainy days. Later I discovered this was Ken Saunders, the Somerset half of the Hampshire/Somerset duo who had founded the Club and given it its hybrid name. The unusual bowling action was the result of a serious back problem which had cut short an illustrious club playing career. The other, less experienced would-be cricketers were spread around the outfield engaged in various activities at which everyone took a turn. I listened intently, there seemed to be so much to learn about a game our own version of which we had played for hours on end under our own devices and our own rules over the 'Players'. Most of the wisdom I heard dispensed directly gainsaid what we had been doing. Those who were fielding were instructed to keep their eye on the ball, bend their knees and above all use two hands whenever possible. Another group was made to execute a bowling action, cartwheel fashion, the leading arm stretched as high and as straight as small limbs would allow, the delivery arm had to come over to brush an, in some cases almost certainly unwashed, ear. All this was first of all choreographed without a ball but then the group graduated to bowling a series of real cricket balls into the boundary fence at the pavilion end, much to the consternation of any birds or other wildlife in the immediate vicinity.

Batting appeared to be incredibly complicated, a perception which stayed with me for a lifetime. It was assumed that those who had presented themselves for coaching were there with the express intention of learning to play 'properly' and so first of all they were made to pick a bat up from the floor in an approved manner, not just grab it, stances were checked, back-lifts were insisted on. Shadow defensive shots, both forward and back, were played, first without a ball and then with a tennis ball delivered by one of the coaches. The bat had to remain straight and close to the body.

Once this had been mastered, the apprentices were allowed to follow through with a flourish, dispatching tennis balls far and wide. It was promised that, once the basic defensive shots had been mastered, they would move on to the more exciting and aggressive strokes such as the pull, the cut and the marvellously expressive hook, which sounded like something more akin to boxing than cricket, but time always seemed to run out before the transition to these promised extravagances could be managed. The stock shot we used at the 'Players', a cross-batted swipe carried out with as much gusto as possible, which ensured that no fielders were ever required on the off-side, an economy which was useful when there was a shortage of available ball-fetchers, never figured in the coaching sessions held by Ron Day, Frank Howes, the more youthful John Bell, who may already by then have been the First Eleven captain, et al.

On the first occasion I sat watching I became aware that one boy, a rather diminutive one compared to the rest, was better than his peers. He seemed able to do all that was required without being shown how to execute these complicated movements. I looked more closely and recognised this prodigy as Micky Bissex who was only one year above me at school. "What's 'e doing 'ere?" I exclaimed loudly within the earshot of the watchful gatekeeper who, since the activities were well underway, had relaxed his screening of under-age participants. "'E's not old enough," I added with as much hard-done by indignation as I could muster. "But he's got a much older brother who's already an established player," retorted hawk-eye and even he must have found this a pathetically inadequate justification, for the lack of conviction in his voice suggested that he wasn't buying his own argument. Only much later did I realise that the real reason for this seemingly preferential treatment, which Rosey could not very well articulate in public, was that Mike Bissex, the future county cricketer and arguably Hampset's most talented cricketing product, was simply so naturally gifted that he was streets ahead of all the others and well able to take care of himself.

Mike Bissex (left) with Micky Dowding, at Bath Cricket Club

I remembered this several years later. I was then at Durham University and Gloucestershire, with Mike in the side, were playing Yorkshire at nearby Middlesbrough. After morning lectures I and a fellow student who was a Yorkshireman and a keen cricketer, Linden Richardson, decided to go to watch and I thought I might perhaps in some way lend support to my Primary School friend, as Yorkshire at the time were riding high and well set to take another championship title. It had rained in the morning and then turned sunny, or at least as sunny as Middlesbrough can manage. An already lively wicket had been turned even more sporty by these conditions and Gloucestershire were finding it tough going against Chris Old and Tony Nicholson. The early order, including some illustrious batsmen, succumbed without much of a fight but Mike and Harold Jarman, better known to us for his footballing exploits, who had more to prove than their more established team-mates, staged something of a fight-back, sustaining some painful blows in the process, armed as they were in those days only with a box and a thigh pad. As I observed this plucky rearguard action I thought back to Rosey and his belief that the younger brother of John Bissex was well able to mix it with the 'big' boys, hard balls or no hard balls. At that earlier time, however, sitting on a bench only able to spectate, the sense of injustice festered and rankled.

From St. Luke's School Odd Down to the MCC Under 25s in Pakistan.
Mike Bissex, third from the right in the back row, is in some illustrious cricketing company including
Mike Brearley, Keith Fletcher, Alan Knott, Derek Underwood, Robin Hobbs and Pat Pocock.

I spent another couple of weeks just watching but itching to be out there taking part and one Tuesday I got my opportunity for the dreaded Rosenburg was not there. If I had then known anything of Rosey's character and pastimes, I would have explained his absence by assuming that he was away heckling some Tory politician at a public meeting, or asking 'awkward' questions, as my mother put it, at a gathering of parents and teachers at St Luke's or penning a forthright letter to *The Chronicle* demanding the reinstatement as soon as possible of the considerable section of Odd Down Playing Fields which had been given over to temporary post-war housing, a campaign he was to wage resolutely for many years. Not only did this dictator want to prevent me from becoming a great cricketer, he wanted to throw me out of house and home as well!

15

I decided that the best ploy was a tried and tested one I had used before, when trying to infiltrate my brother's older friends' games at the 'Players'. I would make myself useful. So, when those in the batting group started to deploy their more expansive shots, I scurried around like a snappy terrier returning tennis balls to the person launching them towards the batsmen, avoiding charging across the square of course which I had already recognised as a hallowed area, tended at that time, as I soon discovered, by the dreaded Rosenburg. When the group to which I had attached myself, which included my brother and others from our estate, moved on to the bowling station I took the bull by the horns and just joined in, first of all cartwheeling my left arm like a whirling dervish high in the air and making sure it brushed my ear, as I had overheard you had to do, if you wanted to be a proper bowler and then delighting in the freedom to hurl at the boundary fence a proper leather cricket ball with a seam, not one of the strange cork things we used at the 'Players' which had always lost any hint of redness and had chunks missing, bitten out by an over-enthusiastic dog who had got to it before a human fielder. When it came to the fielding session I probably resumed my position as a spectator, claiming tiredness and thus started the habit of a lifetime. I had wheedled my way into the main activities, however, and in the weeks that followed I was recognised by the coaches, who encouraged me to join in, thus overruling the self-appointed, way-before-his-time Health and Safety/Child Protection Welfare Officer so beloved by Twenty-First Century bureaucrats.

With our integration into the cricket club's activities a whole new life began. Of course we did not immediately abandon our estate friends or stop using the 'Players' as our all-purpose games area but gradually after school and particularly during the holidays we spent more and more time 'over Hampset', as we told our mother when she, not unreasonably, wanted to know where we were going. This was information which I was constantly to give her right up to marriage almost three decades later.

We discovered that Rosey, who was often at the ground during the day, tending the pitches, was not such an ogre after all, he even became one of our keenest mentors. Sometimes we got to help out in our own small way in his, purely voluntary of course, groundsman's duties. But above all we got to know a huge number of new friends. John Bissex, Dave Walters, Brian Horler, Peter Winch, Pete Allen, Peter Crouch and more were all somewhat older and were already seasoned Hampset boys. About my vintage were Mike Bissex, Bill Barrett, John Nicholas, Bob Staunton, Sam Shearn, Dick Stickells, Foxy Fowler, Vic Oliver, Kenny Bodman and Graham Burman, whose later claim to fame was that he beat Roger Bannister into second place in a school cross-country race at the C.B.B.S (City of Bath Boys' School, now Beechen Cliff), in spite of the fact that he had already taken up a smoking habit to which he was seriously committed.

Only a short while after along came Ron White, the Buckley brothers Dave and Mike, Reg Trim, André Jozwiak, Chris Harding, Dicky Densem and then Kevin Porter, Steve Benjamin and the Szczotko twins swelled the ranks. The Hack brothers covered all three sets. We were progressively joined by others, such as Lyn Morgan, Brian Goodway, Brian Carlin, Pete Mines, Ian Smith, Murray Day, Richard Holmes, Pete Thomas and Colin Sinkins to name but a few. Several young men even came from over the seas to join in, but it was essentially this crop of burgeoning talent which was to sustain the club over several decades and lead it, notwithstanding a few ups and downs, through a golden era in which we competed with all but the very best in club cricket.

The surprising thing is that we were almost without exception Odd Down boys. Sam Shearn lived beyond the boundary and the pale of the Glasshouse and had, therefore, to be considered to be from Combe Down, a disreputable, neighbouring area full of unscrupulous rogues such as its publicans who, according to Odd Down folklore, consistently dispensed watered-down beer in scandalously short measures. John Nicholas lived half way down the hill towards the Bear Flat but otherwise we all lived within a stone's throw of the Bloomfield Rise ground. There are reputedly villages in Lancashire and Yorkshire which can boast of producing a whole string of first-class cricketers, including in some cases several test players and captains, and perhaps also a number of high class footballers but I doubt if there are many places which, within such a short radius, have housed so many accomplished club cricketers as this unlikely corner of Bath. Indeed, you could pick an extremely strong side exclusively from just those who have lived in Bloomfield Drive and Bloomfield Rise. Inevitably we lost a few along the way. Occasionally someone moved away, either to another part of Bath or further afield but this was rare, social mobility not having as yet become a trendy expression.

The most notable fairly early leaver was Brian Buck, who had been one of us from the very early days and who, if his insurance company had not moved him south to the Southampton area, would surely have amassed a pile of runs for the club. Very rarely families from our estate took moving away to a ridiculous extreme and for £10, I never knew if this was per head or per family but either way it was ridiculously cheap, emigrated to Australia never to be seen or heard of again. We also lost a small number to conflicting interests such as other sports, music, drink and, even worse, girls, but overall the drop-out rate was extremely low.

Chris Harding almost went the way of other interests but was rescued in the nick of time. On one occasion, when there was a junior match to be played, he brazenly announced that he was unavailable, as he was going to see a Zorro film. Such flippancy was greeted with incredulity but off he went to the Beau Nash, leaving us to complete the fixture without him. His fascination with the black-clad, masked, heart-in-the-right-place outlaw did not last long and he was soon readmitted to the fold but his fecklessness did not go unpunished for he was known as Zorro forever after. It is wonderful how nicknames, rather a male thing I think, stick for life and of course only a chosen few are party to their origin. "Why do they call you Zorro?" asked his future wife Diane. "It's a long story, dear," was the terse reply, accompanied by a suitably chastened expression. Zorro's youthful errant behaviour was obviously only a momentary lapse for he and Diane are still happily married and fairly recently celebrated his 60th birthday with a bash at a Saltford hostelry at which his own children and the non-cricketing friends and colleagues he has picked up along the way tried hard to puzzle out why a certain bunch of ageing males consistently addressed the man of the moment as a long-faded figure from the silver screen.

Once I had infiltrated the ranks of the practising would-be cricketers I grew quickly in know-how and confidence and I started to acquire proper clothing and equipment. I even got hold of a very much second-hand bat of my own, a size five or six Sykes Slazenger, autographed by Don Bradman and marked with the original retailer's stamp: John Moore's Sports of Bath. This ancient piece of willow had seen much better days but I set about tending it with great care, not because I wanted to use it to any great extent, my lack of interest in batting had probably already kicked in, but because I so enjoyed the maintenance of it. If ever they get round to inviting ordinary people on to *Desert Island Discs* I shall tell Kirsty Young that as a luxury I require an inexhaustible supply of linseed oil and soft rags. In the latter stages of my cricketing career they started to market the latest bats with the slogan 'No need to oil', as if that was an advantage. Didn't these Philistines realise that one of life's great pleasures is to be smelt in the application of raw linseed oil to a cherished piece of willow? I shall wander around the desert island looking for vaguely cricket bat-shaped pieces of wood. They won't need to be willow; bamboo or whatever else is available on the island will do, and I shall happily spend my days caring for them by coating them in a thin layer of that gorgeous, olfactory, yellow liquid, as supplied by Miss Young.

I even fortuitously obtained a proper cricket bag. One day John Bell, by then definitely the leader of the club on the playing side, was going about his business in some country area and happened upon a sale of effects in a village vicarage. Here, for the princely sum of £1, he acquired the reverend gentleman's cricket bag which he passed on to me. It was already fairly ancient, I doubt if the last in a line of incumbents had played for some time. Made predominantly from sturdy canvas, it had two leather handles and four sizeable leather patches at each corner. It also had a locking mechanism to keep the vicar's belonging safe but this had long given up the ghost and there was no way of getting it back into operation. I became incredibly attached to this old bag. Over the years my playing colleagues had a series of new, ever bigger and more exotic objects in which to transport their gear, huge trunks in which you could have buried the dead and latterly kitbags on wheels but I stuck with the vicar's bag. Finally it developed quite serious holes and essential items of kit, such as pens to do the crossword with, went missing. Finally I had to get a new bag, a hideous, heavy-duty, plastic object, plastered with the maker's logo but with no character. I could not bring myself to part with my beloved green bag and it still resides in the loft, ready in case the MCC are ever short at the last minute of a left-arm spinner slightly past his sell-by date.

With my kit assembled from a range of different sources I was at last ready for the summons, if and when it came, to play in a proper match for Hampset Juniors. As it happened, I did not have to wait long to figure in a club fixture – straight into the First Eleven.

Welcome to Odd Down

My introduction to Hampset was lukewarm but my welcome to Odd Down was downright hostile. I was born, a veritable baby-boomer, in the middle of 1946 at home, which was then more often the case, in South View Road, East Twerton, a real Bathonian, therefore, in the Wife of Bath's terms, at the house of my maternal grandparents. As with so many couples, my parents' lives had been completely thrown upside down by the war. Pre-war they were both employed by the Co-op, my father as a grocer in one of the shops which were dotted around Bath, and my mother as an office worker in the local headquarters in Westgate Buildings. They had been married just prior to the conflict and my father went off 'to do his bit' shortly afterwards. A spell of home leave led to my brother's appearance in 1942 but mine was delayed by further posting, injury, the contracting of malaria, repatriation and a period of rehabilitation in Chertsey.

My maternal grandparents outside the place of my birth, 8 South View Road, East Twerton, on the occasion of a Jubilee, Coronation or royal wedding. Grandfather looks set to join in the celebrations at the Charmbury Arms at the end of the street in Brook Road. Grandmother, on the other hand, might be more intent on discouraging such frivolity. Cat unknown.

The house in South View Road, which was owned by my grandparents, a most unusual thing for people of modest means in those days, remained in the family until the death of my Aunty Floss in her 94th year well into the twenty-first century. It had survived the dropping of an errant bomb at the bottom of its long garden which backed onto the Lower Bristol Road and from which one had a close-up view of the town's gas-holders, and over which the steam locomotives of the Somerset and Dorset Railway huffed and puffed in their literally uphill struggle towards Combe Down and Midford. The house itself was small and still lit in my infant years by dim gas mantles, it had no proper kitchen or bathroom and there was an outside 'safe' with a door made of fine iron mesh in which meat and other perishables were kept. Life must have been uncomfortable and above all cramped for my grandparents, my parents, a young boy and a baby.

Not surprisingly we must have been near the top of the council housing list and sure enough in January 1947 we were placed in one of the spanking new prefabs, erected as a temporary solution to the post-war housing shortage, on an estate which had rather controversially been sited on half of Odd Down Playing Fields, an extensive area of municipal pitches for games such as football, cricket, hockey and for a brief period polo on bicycles, a poor-man's version of the real thing which did not really catch on.

For the next 21 years I did not go upstairs to bed for home was to be no. 1 Chelwood Drive, the very first of the bungalows, made from corrugated, asbestos concrete panels, as you turned into the estate; the space it occupied is now a section of the car park of the partly restored playing fields. The prefab had two bedrooms, a quite spacious sitting-room with an enclosed coal fire which provided copious amounts of hot water from a tank located behind it, and a kitchen, which, if not 'fitted' in the modern sense of the term, was well appointed. My mother for some reason always added a diminutive suffix and referred to this room as the kitchenette, although it was far bigger than the kitchen space she had left in South View Road.

Soon after I had taken up my teaching appointment at Dauntsey's at the end of the seventies I accompanied a school trip to the museum district of West London. The pupils were allowed to choose which museum they wished to visit and I found myself accompanying those who had selected the Science Museum, I'm sure not out of choice, since the wonders of science have always remained unfathomable and of little interest to me. I wandered rather aimlessly from room to room and then to my amazement found myself – in our kitchen! The typical prefab kitchen(ette) had been reconstructed behind a large glass screen, presumably to exemplify the ingenuity of post-war planners. It all came flooding back to me, for here, all polished up and gleaming were all the familiar fixtures in their light green and yellow with red switches and buttons, the Belling cooker on which were produced our meat and two veg meals and where, somewhat less appetizingly, our pants were boiled in a large saucepan, there being, of course, no washing machine, not even a twin-tub. In the corner by the window which looked onto the 'Players' was the shelf where our two cats curled up in blissful, warm, feline harmony. I did not quite recognise the cardboard cut-out figure of a fifties housewife in her smart, floral pinny. Peering through the glass was an audience, mostly of young people, gazing with a certain air of condescending amusement at what no doubt seemed to them a fairly primitive and inadequate arrangement. I scuttled away with a feeling that I had been in some sort of freak show.

In front of each of the neat little detached houses was a small grassed area but behind there was a larger garden and ours was even bigger than the rest, the reward for being the first in the rank. The homes and gardens were separated one from the other by only a few flimsy strands of wire but residents soon installed their own privet hedges or fences made of neat wooden palisades to give greater privacy. A few flowers or bushes might be allowed at the front. Our door, for example, was flanked by two large arrays of Michaelmas daisies, but the back garden was given over, in almost every case to the more serious activity of growing vegetables, berries and even fruit.

Many of those who lived in the prefabs for some length of time became very fond of them. This affection was shown, when they were eventually pulled down, by the fact that a lot of residents, including my mother, wanted to keep the front door. In our case it was transported the short distance to the new abode in Corston View and integrated into a form of back porch, always referred to by my mother as 'the lobby', constructed as a buffer against the ever present wind. For many years I attempted to maintain this door so that it consisted more of filler than of wood and was held together by a mixture of hope and inexpertly applied Dulux.

At the bottom of the gardens of the houses on the left hand side of Chelwood Drive ran a very tall, stout, metal chain-link fence, designed to keep people out of the playing fields when they were closed, for the area was subject to strict opening hours. However, this defensive stockade had an Achilles heel in the far corner of our garden where it met a low stone wall which separated us from the long, narrow garden and the cottage which faced directly onto the main road and which was initially inhabited by the Maggs family before they coughed up a small sum and emigrated to Canada. It was over this wall that we were able to lead teams of estate children intent on enjoying games of cricket and football, even when the 'Players' was not open for official business.

Living as they were in less than ideal conditions, my parents were no doubt looking forward to being rehoused in the prefab, even if the new accommodation was seen only as temporary, and the move duly took place in January 1947, when I was just six months old. Unfortunately, however, the transfer from balmy Twerton to bracing Odd Down coincided with the onset of the most extreme winter conditions experienced since ice-age mammoths roamed the southern heights above the valley of the river Avon. I was apparently kept indoors for the whole of the next three months until the wintry grip was finally released. This Odd Down baptism by snow and ice had a profound effect on my mother who had spent her whole life until then in the more temperate zone of East Twerton. Forever onwards she opined at regular intervals that "it is always cold on Odd Down" and for the rest of her life she always wore a hat outdoors and often indoors as well.

My mother pictured in the early 1930s at Mower's Studios of 19a Westgate Street, Bath. The photograph has been made into a postcard, as seems to have been quite common at the time. Perhaps people sent out pictures of themselves with news, a primitive form of Facebook. Living in the balmy climate of East Twerton, Miss Ada Beatrice Martin feels able to pose hatless.

Decades later the rigours of Odd Down have persuaded her to wear a hat even when indoors with her thumb-sucking granddaughter.

When she died my best friend of the early Odd Down years, Mike Hillman, whom I had not seen for years, attended the funeral and, since he had rarely seen my mother with her head uncovered, asked in all seriousness if she was to be buried in her hat. We'd certainly toyed with the idea but in the end we simply kept her last example of functional, protective millinery, a light-green affair which sat, firmly secured by a hatpin flat against the head, with other effects in the loft.

As someone who had spent almost the whole of the first half of her life without the cushioning support of the Welfare State and the National Health Service, well-being was quite a preoccupation with my mother. The best form of preventative medicine was to be found in the consumption of the water in which cabbage had been boiled and, since this vegetable was a major part of our staple diet, this elixir was constantly available. I cannot say that I ever managed to drink this greenish, foul-smelling liquid but it seems to have worked because it kept her without any serious health problems for all but the last few days of her ninety-year existence. It was also necessary to sleep well, to keep out of draughts, to keep one's bowels open and, above all, to avoid allowing one's extremities, in the shape of one's head and feet, to become either cold or wet, hence the ever-present hat. For some reason, to permit one's feet to get even slightly damp was to court all sorts of deadly repercussions. To ensure that the bowels were kept open with what was indelicately described as 'a good turn-out' she sometimes had to resort to a laxative which came in the form of dark chocolate and was only to be consumed in the smallest of portions. For the whole of the rest of my life, when on occasions in polite society, after an event such as a church service, a school play, the annual sports or prize-giving, it has been remarked that the organisers had been gratified by 'a good turn-out', I have never been able to suppress my mirth, usually to the consternation of those making the judgement.

On one occasion, when I was still very young, I happened upon a box of the chocolate-like laxative and greedily ate a whole bar of it. Needless to say, I spent the next few days chained to the lavatory pan and broke all records for the number of times I 'had been', although what emerged was in no way solid, consisting mostly of a stream of black liquid, not unlike the secretions of loose-bowelled cows. This incident was related at regular intervals for years to come, always much to my teenage or adult embarrassment and discomfiture and the rider was always added that "for many years afterwards our Malc never had a day's illness", cited as proof positive of the beneficial effect of being 'regular'. Much less devastating was the consumption of cod liver oil and malt, an essential for immediate post-war children. No doubt this would have been unpalatable without the malt but with the additive I actually came quite to like it, which was just as well because we had to have a dessertspoonful a day; the cats were allowed to lick the spoon and they both lived to about twenty so it must have had something going for it.

Once the snowdrifts had disappeared our lives on Odd Down could begin in earnest. My father was back at his Co-op grocery job, my brother started school and my mother and I were left at home in the prefab. There was still no question of going back to work for married women and mothers, although the country had been willing enough to make use of them when the men were away at war. I was now allowed out, but 'well togged-up' in view of the fresh weather, and it was here in the garden that I learned to read, courtesy of the Bristol Omnibus Company. Odd Down's umbilical cord to Bath at the time was the no. 11 double-decker bus which ran from Larkhall through the city centre to Odd Down. A single-decker no. 6 made a lateral assault on the down via Rush Hill but it ran less frequently and had the reputation for being less than reliable for punctuality. On the side of the buses were displayed large advertising slogans which I memorised and read out. "Beer is best," I would exclaim and "Guinness is good for you", to remain in a bibulous mood. "Sunlight Soap is the best in the world," some no. 11s proclaimed from their lofty side panels and the rather intriguing "Aberthaw Cement". In those post-war reconstruction days did people commonly pop round to their local corner shop and pick up a bag of cement?

Double-decker buses were not the only mobile reading flashcards available. In those days, notwithstanding the modern vans speeding to deliver goods ordered at the click of a mouse, there were far more retail delivery vans buzzing around and they were all emblazoned with their owner's name and business, leading to the constant "What does that say?" question for my patient mother to answer. Fascinatingly all these traders seemed to be 'purveyors' of something, purveyors of choice-cut meats, of fresh fish, of cakes and pastries and many other products. But the most interesting motors with writing on them, other than buses, were municipal vehicles, such as dustcarts and road sweepers, which, as I soon learnt to read out, all bore the owner's name and address, in case they got lost: Jared E Dixon. Town Clerk. Guildhall. Bath, along with a serial number. Who was this fortunate person who got to play with all these vans and lorries when they went home in the evening? The E must surely stand for something grand to go with the unusual first name, certainly not a mere Eric or Ernie, more likely an Ebenezer or a Eustace.

It was not long before I was taken for rides inside the learn-to-read material and here there were more notices to repeat: 'Please tender exact fare and state destination', 'No smoking' (on the lower deck) and 'No spitting' (all over the bus). At some stage the widespread habit of expectorating in public must have waned of its own accord, for the notice banning this unfortunate activity became less and less common. I did once see, on the side of a cathedral no less, a sign saying 'Défense d'uriner', but that was France of course where they need to be told that sort of thing. We got on at the back of the bus and I much preferred the top deck, although at times this area was wreathed in clouds of pungent smoke and the floor was covered in cigarette butts which had to be stubbed out on little silver, metal squares attached to the back of the seats, put there precisely for that purpose. We were greeted by a (usually) cheerful conductor who later came round to dispense tickets from a wooden board reminiscent of an elongated mousetrap on which were impaled tickets of various colours to serve different purposes: adult single, child return, etc. There was no question of any intimacy with the driver who, cocooned in his cab at the front, wrestling with the controls of a green monster so much less easy to manage than its later counterparts, remained in contact with his co-operative by a series of bell messages: one for stop, two for go. From our vantage point on the upper deck the no. 11 bus route soon became very familiar, or at least half of it did. We knew nothing of the leg from the centre to Larkhall, which might as well have been New Zealand or the other side of the moon, because there was never any question of us venturing to anywhere so remote. The journey to Odd Down began at Bog Island or, in more genteel parlance, North Parade. Buses bearing advertisements, such as those already mentioned or ones for glutinous brown substances such as Bovril or Camp Coffee, an unpalatable concoction of chicory essence which my aunty Floss actually seemed to like, but then she also drank UHT milk, so her taste buds had definitely been affected by something along the line, would have a rest and a chat at this city centre circle still known to Bathonians as Bog Island. The public toilets in the middle, which gave the area its name, access to which was gained by a set of stairs which spiralled down into a realm of marble appliances with shining brass accessories attended to by men in brown coats and constantly bathed in the smell of bleach and disinfectant, have long gone.

Our faithful no. 11 would then set off from base camp, skirting the back of the Abbey and turning left at the end of Cheap Street, it passed a long-demolished hotel guarded by two huge stone lions and descended Southgate Street, not as it is now with its relatively tasteful, latest rebuilding, nor even in its hideous preceding version, but the one before that. It bisected two cinemas, the Odeon and the Forum, the latter more upmarket, as it had a commissionaire who patrolled outside in a green uniform with gold braid. At the bottom of town it went over the Old Bridge, as long as it wasn't flooded, as happened relatively often, and under the railway bridge in whose arches several artisans plied their trade and on up towards the Bear Flat, passing Oldfield Secondary Modern Boys' School on the right. The bus was already a little out of breath after the long, sweeping uphill journey to the Bear Flat, a plateau, from which emanated roads at right angles all named after poets and literary figures. Here it could have a fleeting rest and took the opportunity to gird its loins for the task ahead. The chance to catch its breath was short-lived for it soon branched off right, bidding farewell to its no. 3 colleagues who took the slightly less steep, more effete road towards Combe Down. At first the foothills around St Luke's Church were not too difficult but the real ascent began after Hatfield Road. A series of crashing gear changes, in spite of frantic double-declutching, attested to the increasing steepness of the climb. To the left rose up some very uneven fields, the 'tumps', where Odd Down's most notorious killer, John Straffen, had done in one of his young girl victims. I remember being taken rather ghoulishly by my mother to gaze at this unfortunate scene soon after the dire deed had been committed, although I was more interested in the two large conker trees which rose up on the opposite side, the source of our armoury when the conker season came round. I couldn't have been totally indifferent though because the 'tumps' was never somewhere we felt like venturing to play. Onwards and upwards the gallant bus sweated. From an early age I was fascinated by the name of one house which clung precariously to the hillside, Keewaydin, long before I had ever heard of Longfellow or knew that the house was in fact the residence of our future coach at Hampset, Ken Saunders. "It's a nice house," admitted my mother, "with a lovely view, but I wouldn't like to live there, think of the wind (bad for the health) and the steep drop." On the bus panted to Bloomfield Crescent, the set of houses which some eighteenth century architects had designed in the right shape but, in some disorientation, had placed on the wrong hill, with the driver praying that nobody would ring the bell to stop, thus necessitating a hill start from scratch. Finally we reached the crest of the hill and the stop where we alighted, after which our steed could bowl its way happily along to the Burnt House Inn where it turned and enjoyed a well earned rest before plunging back towards the city.

When out for a walk on a summer's day in the countryside beyond Odd Down hats were still de rigueur for Mrs Johnson and her boys.

Streets ahead of the game

When I was a little older I was able to graduate from the garden to the streets of the estate to play, first with friends of my own age like Mike Hillman and Gerry Tidcombe, but then also with older boys of my brother's vintage when they were available after school, at weekends and in the holidays. A lot is made of the difference in play patterns between those of my generation and children of today's computer age. Certainly we had a lot more freedom but there was very little traffic around the prefabs, only delivery vans, bicycles and perhaps the odd motor-cycle, because no-one on the estate had the means to run a car. Also I was lucky enough to have a brother almost five years older and who could be charged with looking after me. The first form of locomotion was a pedal car with the hackneyed registration of RU18. If you could get hold of two sets of wheels from a pram or a pushchair, a couple of planks of wood and a stout piece of rope, a 'trolley' could be manufactured on which hours of fun could be had, taking it in turns to be pushed around the prefab-lined streets. Games included hop-scotch, hide-and-seek, piggy-in-the-middle and the first rudimentary attempts at cricket against a lamppost with a piece of wood and a tennis ball. Even with such paltry equipment you could imagine yourself as the English test team fighting off the challenge of the three Ws, Walcott, Worrell and Weekes. Scores from these imaginary Test Matches were dutifully recorded in a customised scorebook. Innings totals were rarely anywhere near those of the real thing. On one occasion an over-zealous pull to leg by Raman Subba Row, aka MKF Johnson, resulted in the improvised bat flying out of my hand and through our lounge window. Match (and those scheduled for the next few weeks) abandoned through confiscation of equipment under parental order – something which, to my knowledge, has never happened in the professional circles we were trying to ape.

Real liberation came when we all acquired bikes which, somehow or other, our parents managed to get for us. To begin with we rode around the estate which was sort of pear-shaped stretching at its bulbous bottom down to Wellsway and the Red Lion. Here a couple of pathways meant that pedestrians, or juvenile cyclists, the latter not always the favourites of the former, could cut through to widen their horizons, one gave access to the Red Lion roundabout and the other to Sammy's corner. I believe this junction of Midford Road and Wellsway, just below the outer wall of St Martin's Hospital is still known by this name, although the present generation probably does not understand why.

Sammy was a little old cobbler, presumably named Samuel, who plied his trade in a wooden shack on the north side of the road. His shoe-mending shed has long gone, a modern house has been erected on the small plot of land on which it stood, but his name lives on in the unofficial name for the area; Sammy's immortality is afforded to relatively few in any walk of life. We rarely had to avail ourselves of Sammy's expertise, as my father had learned the same skills during his post-conflict rehabilitation, along with the ability to make soft toys from felt and other materials, a happy combination of the functional and the aesthetic.

Mother, sons and a large cat at the back of the prefab. A similar window suffered the indignity of a bat flying through it.

The perimeter of the estate was all Chelwood Drive and the rows of houses which went in neat lines across the middle of the pear-formed Winscombe Road. Also in the middle of the estate was an electric sub-station which we referred to as the 'Power House' and which we were banned from entering, literally on pain of death. Round and round these streets we rode, often with a folded up cigarette packet stuck between the spokes to make a clicking noise which must have been intensely annoying for all those who could hear it. Senior Service packets were highly prized as the most likely to produce the loudest din.

Soon we had exhausted the attraction of riding in pear-shaped figures around our own realm and, on strict instructions to be careful, we were allowed to pedal further afield. First of all our rides took in the roads in the immediate vicinity; it was on one of these expeditions of discovery that we first became aware of the existence of Hampset Cricket Club.

Venturing ever further from base we got as far as the Glasshouse junction, a sort of Checkpoint Charlie between us and the uncivilised hordes of Combe Down. We reached the Burnt House Inn and beyond to Kilkenny Woods in which branches and sticks could be found, from which we made home-made, Robin Hood patented bows and arrows, lethal weapons if they fell into irresponsible hands. In the same general area we happened upon the Fuller's Earth works which were still in operation at the time, and from the road to Combe Hay you could access the opening to one of the mines. The exact nature of the obviously precious substance hewn from deep under our feet was a mystery to us and the pit was really scary, even for such adventurers as ourselves, hardened as we were by familiarity with the experiences of the Famous Five and the Secret Seven and years of attendance at 'Saturday morning pictures' at the Odeon. We rarely took more than a few steps into the darkness, following railway tracks on which ran trucks which carried to the surface the valuable commodity, which men risked everything to garner, before we found some reason why we must turn tail and regain the light and relative security.

As we got older we got even more adventurous and cycled considerable distances. We made it as far as Englishcombe, Priston, Limpley Stoke and the castle at Farleigh Hungerford. Then we got really ambitious and decided we would cycle as far as Weston-super-Mare, after all it didn't take _that_ long on the train! We got as far as Blagdon before common sense made us turn round, but even that is amazing. However little legs got to pedal that far on bikes with gears which were far from sophisticated is remarkable as the same journey in adulthood in a car is quite tiring.

On all these bike rides we went armed with a bicycle pump, a couple of cheese or jam sandwiches, a bottle of Corona and, most importantly, our I-Spy books to record our discoveries en route. Between us we had just about the complete series of these little books which were published in categories such as birds, cars, trees, flowers, churches and other buildings, and many others, which proved to be a marvellous way of opening our eyes to the world around us. Upon encountering some nominated example of the set in any particular book, each one accompanied by a picture and some descriptive notes to help you identify it, you recorded your new discovery by stating when and where you had seen it and gained points for having done so. Some things were worth more points than others, depending on their rarity, thus a Morris Minor was not worth as much as a Maserati, an orchid brought more credit than a primrose or a cowslip. Once the book was complete or you had reached a certain number of points you sent it off to Big Chief I-Spy, who also conducted a regular I-Spy column in the _News Chronicle_, and he sent you an appropriate feather to add to your Indian Chief's headdress. I do not know how closely Big Chief I-Spy scrutinised the entries and there was probably considerable scope for putting in imagined sightings and fraudulent claims but I do not think such cheating was at all widespread. There was little point in pretending that you had seen a buzzard at Noad's Corner or a tropical palm tree in a garden in windswept Chelwood Drive. I am told that I-Spy books have recently been relaunched by Michelin, I'm not sure how they will go down with modern youngsters but I wish them well for they provided us with hours of interest and instruction.

The snows of winter, which appeared quite regularly, sometimes in copious amounts though without ever reaching the huge proportions which had coincided with our arrival on Odd Down, provided many further possibilities for amusement. There were the obvious snowball fights, attempts at sledging in a field near Entry Hill, and the sculpting of snowmen. But the greatest fun was to be had in the making of a 'slide'. Once the snow had been compacted in the middle of the road, by careful and persistent rubbing it could be turned into a shining strip of sheet ice, which over time could be made longer and longer. Once a reasonable amount of slippery surface had been created, if you took a run at it you could glide in an upright position, with knees bent like an expert skier, at some considerable speed over however long the slide stretched. As long as a thaw did not set in, the best ones could eventually be made tens of metres in length, great fun for the experienced sliders. Our slides, however, were a lethal hazard for pedestrians who were often forced by piled up snow on the pavements to walk in the road, and for the small number of motor vehicles which inched their way painfully around the snowy roads, their dim headlights unable to pick out the man-made (or boy-made) danger in front of them. Some of these cars and vans did not play the game and donned chains which may have wrecked their tyres but gave them greater temporary freedom to move around at more normal speeds and which, unfortunately from our point of view, destroyed a slide which had taken many hours to perfect. Conversely the vehicles most at risk from the trap we had laid for them, particularly in the darkness of a winter evening or night, were motor-cycles, which habitually skidded and even capsized on making contact with our stretch of gleaming ice, much to our misplaced amusement.

Days and weeks either side of November 5th were also taken up by activities some of which cause us, as more sensible adults looking back on childhood pursuits, a certain amount of embarrassed shame. Bangers, which could be bought quite easily at any age for 1d or 2d each, were placed in cans or bottles or thrown around with gay, irresponsible abandon. Rockets were set off with dangerous, low-flying trajectories. Even news of Roger Bruton, a schoolfriend, blowing the finger off one of his hands when playing about with a firework in his dad's shed in Bloomfield Drive, did not deter us from these foolhardy activities. More innocently a guy was usually made from old clothes begged from parents and stuffed with straw which had probably already served its time as bedding in our rabbits' cages and thus gave off an unmistakeable odour. Even the best examples rarely earned many pennies when the effigy was put strategically on display, a cardboard money-seeking notice hung around its floppy neck, at the bus stop on the top road to catch those alighting from their day's business in town. "Bugger off" was not an unusual reaction to the alms-seeking request. The few coins which were gained in this way were immediately ploughed back into the purchase of yet more bangers to hurl about indiscriminately. Wood and other combustible material was gathered over the weeks leading up to Guy Fawkes Night, which had to be protected against pilfering by rival fire builders, and the bonfire was duly lit on the green outside our house on the appointed evening. Sometimes, if there had been a lot of rain, the conflagration had to be encouraged with a splash of paraffin, acquired from what had been stored to fuel some family's Valor heater. Modern Health and Safety Officers would have had a fit at the activities surrounding November 5th on 1950s Odd Down. Present-day children are surely more sensibly taken to organised displays by their parents.

If the weather was at all conducive we were outside but sometimes even we were forced indoors, either chez Mike Hillman or in our house. It must have been way back then that Mike realised that my mother, still not immune to the Odd Down climate, was inseparable from her hat, a memory which stuck with him for years to come. For indoor amusement we had a wealth of pooled resources to choose from: jigsaws, dinky toys, lead soldiers, Meccano sets, comics, matchbox labels, cigarette cards and stamps. The latter were a never-ending source of education and fascination. The recently departed king, his immediate predecessors and the new, young queen seemed to figure on the stamps of most countries of the world which we acquired from a variety of sources and which we duly stuck into our albums with gummed hinges. One king, a gentleman with slicked down hair, only appeared for a short time and our mother explained that he had been forced to abdicate, which sounded rather painful. Most albums had a map of the world in the front to help identify the provenance of the latest acquisition, and we noted with some pride that much of the globe was coloured red. Each country had a page, or a series of pages for those most likely to yield a greater number of these postal tokens, and under each heading there was almost certainly an explanatory snapshot of the place in question. Thus we were told, for example, that Andorra was "a miniature republic in the Pyrenees under the suzerainty (they expected a broad vocabulary in young collectors then) of France and Spain" and that Belgium was "a kingdom in Western Europe with an area of 11,750 square miles. Capital: Brussels." Germany was rather dismissed as "a large territory in Northern Central Europe. At present under Allied occupation." 'Serve 'em right,' we no doubt jingoistically thought. The queen and her husband and her late father adorned stamps from many exotic sounding places, many of them now consigned to history: Aden, Ascension, Bechuanaland, Basutoland, Gold Coast, Nyasaland, the Pitcairn Islands and Southern Rhodesia. A portly man with a cigar also figured quite regularly. Our stamps and those from our empire were soberly square or rectangular shaped but some more showy ones from unknown places such as the 'Magyar Republic' were ostentatiously round, triangular or even diamond shape. In a small shop in town you could buy stamps of individual countries or themed packets on subjects such as birds, trains, sportsmen etc which might contain items on the specified subject from all sorts of locations and were thus the most likely to contain surprises such as wombats from Australia, tigers from India or locusts from Chad. 'Doublers' could always be swapped. A Stanley Gibbons stamp catalogue was viewed as a precious commodity and the latest version became a much desired Christmas present.

Fortunately indoor games and pastimes could still be of a sporting nature. Cardboard football league ladders with slots into which could be positioned the teams in all four leagues (1st, 2nd, 3rd division north, 3rd division south), a free gift at the beginning of the season from the *News of the World*, were scrupulously kept up to date, as soon as the Sunday paper arrived. The revised league positions could be made even earlier if we managed to get a *Pink 'Un* or a *Green 'Un*, the local Saturday evening sports papers dutifully brought to us on Odd Down by an ageing, squat figure hunched over from years of lugging heavy paper bags around, that is bags containing papers. This figure alighted from the no. 11 bus every Saturday evening, carrying his variegated publications with the ink still wet off the press, and clutching a leather bag into which he dropped the 1d coins proffered by eager, small hands. A few years later it was with even greater anticipation that we rushed to get these broadsheets to see if there was an account in them of the previous weekend's Hampset fixtures in which, if we had done anything at all meritorious, our names might figure. It was in one such account that Reg Trim famously appeared as Red Grim, the typesetter presumably having served his apprenticeship on the *Guardian* or perhaps in those days it still had its preceding *Manchester* in the title. Because of this, pink in journalistic terms will for ever be associated for me with sport, rather than finance, and perhaps explains my search on every trip to France for *L'Equipe* in which one commonly finds out how things are going in the Mexican basketball league or the Finnish synchronised swimming semi-finals.

As far as the Saturday football results were concerned, we might even have pre-empted the arrival of our gnarled newsvendor by scribbling down the scores from *Sports Report* which was broadcast at 5pm on the Light Programme, heralded each week by the jaunty music still used to this day. Having learned the results by any of these methods, we delighted in moving into their correct, up-to-date position in the league the narrow strips of cardboard which represented places of which we knew nothing other than that they had a football team: Accrington Stanley might have leapfrogged Hartlepool United or Preston North End stayed in the same position after a goalless draw with Bolton Wanderers. Seeking these places on a map in an atlas showed that most were to be found in the barren wastes of the north of England where people wore clogs and existed on a diet of bread and dripping. The week to week position of Bristol Rovers caused us the most pride or disquiet depending on their latest fortunes. Non-league Bath City did not merit a cardboard mention. For us the interest lay entirely in the sporting achievements of the various sides, but mid-week our tables were put to more serious and practical work as my father pored over them trying to forecast the outcomes of the coming weekend's fixtures. He filled in his pools coupon accordingly with eight draws correctly, he hoped, prognosticated and thus would earn us a fortune. In those days they did not even have to be score draws, just any old draws would do, but his system, if he had one, never worked and in this regard our Sunday newspaper donated league tables never had the desired effect. In increasing desperation he began to ask us our opinion, wrongly believing us to be experts, but we could not come up trumps either. Perhaps any sort of success would have turned us into inveterate gamblers, so every cloud really does have a silver lining.

Endless games of cricket, Test Matches or County Games, all scrupulously recorded in a series of exercise/scorebooks, were played simply using two six or eight-sided pencils. These were shaved off at one end and marked either with runs scored or with a method of dismissal. The first was rolled over a smooth surface and runs recorded for a batsman until the dreaded W for wicket appeared on the uppermost, pared off side of the pencil. The second then came into play and the way in which the batsman had met his doom was hit upon – caught, stumped etc. The entry was made in the scorebook and the next batsman took his stance at the imaginary crease. I believe it is now possible to buy a commercially produced, polished version of this game but nothing could quite replace our customised pencils.

Subbuteo came a bit later. We had played a bit at home with a couple of teams but it became a really serious business once I had acquired my new Hampset friends. Any bout of inclement weather sent us scurrying from the club usually two or three doors down to Bill Barrett's long-suffering mother's front room where for hours intense, finger-flicked football matches were played out. Between us we had assembled several teams in their distinctive strips. A particularly local enthusiast could pretend that the black and white stripes of Newcastle United were those of Bath City. The distinctive hockey-like blue and white quarters of Bristol Rovers were another favourite but I must say I was above all fond of Blackpool, not only that I might step vicariously into the studded boots of Matthews, Mortensen et al, but mostly because of their tangerine shirts, something which has not changed with their long overdue return to the top flight in 2010. The pundits say that Blackpool and their West Country manager are destined to go straight back down. I hope they're wrong.

Our young lives were thus spent around the streets and roads of Odd Down and in each other's houses. Our activities were as exclusively all-male as those of any secret society. By the law of averages some of our ever-expanding group must have had sisters but there was never any question of girls being included in our pastimes. Occasionally we were aware of a set of that other type of children skipping, either individually or in groups with an extra long rope, or playing 'two-ball' against a wall, a game in which, for girls, they displayed a commendable amount of coordination and ball sense. But for the most part we simply ignored them. These female games always, it appeared, had to be accompanied by shrill chants and songs with utterly nonsensical lyrics:

Nebuchadnezzar the King of the Jews
Sold his wife for a pair of shoes
When the shoes began to pinch
Nebuchadnezzar began to flinch

When the shoes began to wear
Nebuchadnezzar began to swear
When the shoes began to leak
Nebuchadnezzar began to squeak

When the shoes began to crack
Nebuchadnezzar said "Take them back" (fortissimo)
The moral of this story's true
If your wife you want to lose
Don't sell her for a pair of shoes

Or the less moralistic :

Cinderella dressed in yella
Went upstairs to kiss her fella
Made a mistake and kissed a snake
How many doctors did it take?

Ann Maggs, sister of Ronnie, who lived over the stone wall which divided our garden from theirs and Bloomfield Road beyond, once tried to corner our attention by offering to show us what lay beneath her serge knickers in the coal hole which abutted the Maggs' cottage but her suggestion was spurned. This rejection must have rankled, for not long after she persuaded her family to emigrate to Canada, a far-flung land where perhaps her attractions received more sympathetic interest. We remained entirely unaware of female charms and attributes until the young ladies of CBGS (City of Bath Girls' School), which now goes by some other name, of the Bath High School, which has now amalgamated with another lady-forming institution, and of the Convent School, which no longer exists, who shared the no. 11 bus with us as we made our way to our respective secondary schools, began to develop protuberances in the region of their chests and to allow their skirts to inch slowly upwards above the knee to reveal stretches of thigh, of which hitherto we had been largely unaware. The nuns in the Convent School, which was situated more or less opposite Bath Cricket Club, on the corner of North Parade and Pulteney Road, were no doubt assiduous in preserving the modesty and demure nature of their charges but even they were ingenious in displaying the increasing attraction of their developing shape. These Roman Candles, as they were disparagingly termed, bewitched and beguiled as much as their namesakes which sparkled and fizzed on Bonfire Night. The city centre lost one of its prettiest sights when the Convent School closed its doors and became some sort of court, removing from the handsome streets equally elegant young ladies in their maroon uniforms and cream boaters.

Over 'the Players'

Notwithstanding our predilection for being outside with friends, there were inevitably times when we were just at home en famille. No television of course, the wireless reigned supreme. I was frightened to death by serials such as *Journey into Space* and *The Day of the Triffids*. *Take it from Here* and *The Goon Show* kept us amused but the abiding memory is of winter evenings with all four of us, my parents, my brother Chris and I, listening intently to the adventures of the detective Paul Temple. We were glued to the set for every episode, each of which was introduced by the hauntingly appropriate music of the Coronation Scot. This would certainly have to be my first piece of music on Miss Young's desert island. The inevitable cliff-hanging ending of each week's programme with Paul and/or his long-suffering wife yet again left in mortal danger kept us intrigued and worried until the next instalment rescued him/ her/them from his/her/their latest predicament. When a TV did eventually appear it never kept our attention as fully as this, the radio's finest production.

Before the advent of the inevitable television we were entertained for a short while by another source of moving pictures, home movies, provided by a projector which had seen better days and which my father had secured from somewhere and reels of film rented from Cyril Howe's in Cheap Street. These films flickered across an improvised screen, the projector regularly broke down or the film simply snapped. Classic short silent movies, at which we split our sides, were our favourites but I cannot remember a session lasting in its entirety without some unscheduled interruption. It must surely have been the frustrations of these technical hitches which led my parents, at some sacrifice, to follow most other families around us and acquire a huge brown cabinet in which sat a small television screen and which took up a considerable part of the lounge.

The arrival of what was to become a dominant part of almost everyone's lives did not stop us from going out to see films at the cinema. I can remember *The Adventures of Robin Hood* and *The Battle of the River Plate*. The film *Rock Around the Clock* introduced us to Bill Haley, the Platters, who remained firm favourites, and to music in general. These films were seen at The Odeon, the Beau Nash or The Forum cinemas in town but, rather surprisingly in view of its proximity to our grandparents' home which we used to visit often, I can only recall once going to The Scala in Oldfield Park before it metamorphosed into a Co-op store. That was one of the first indications of the demise of the cinema, strangled by the ever growing popularity of the boxes invading people's houses. This sole outing was to see *Smiley*, who was the eponymous hero of a film about an Australian 10-year-old whose determination to buy a bicycle led him into a series of misadventures. But our most regular visits to the cinema came in the form of 'Saturday morning pictures'. A shilling was ample for a return ticket on the workhorse no. 11 bus, entrance to the Odeon and an ice lolly or a bag of popcorn. The programme always had several facets: a cartoon or two, a short documentary, perhaps a B movie suitable for children and the finale, the current serial with its suspense-filled ending designed to bring us back the following week. Looking back now I wonder what it would have been like to have watched one of these serials in its entirety at one sitting, littered as they were at regular intervals with these terror-filled moments of suspense. No doubt it would have been an emotional experience akin to a ride on a fairground roller-coaster. The Saturday morning session was accompanied throughout by childish laughter, shrieks and gasps of alternating excitement and fear, there being no adults or courting couples snogging on the back row to shush us up. Some semblance of order was kept by harassed usherettes who must have seen this as the nadir of their week just as we looked upon it as the zenith. Each week we emerged blinking into the light of a bustling Saturday lunchtime, punch drunk from the gamut of emotions we had just experienced. For me it was only secondary school, with the need to attend on Saturday mornings, which finally put a stop to this regular date with the silver screen, although it did not last much longer anyway, another victim for the dreaded television.

Somewhat more tranquil was our growing interest in train-spotting. Visits were made quite frequently to our maternal grandparents (we had no paternal ones, they had departed this earth when my father himself was still a child). Soon there was just my grandfather since, when I was about four years old, my one existing grandmother came down one morning, had her boiled egg, sat down for a moment and didn't wake up. My brother went to the funeral but I was deemed to be too young and had to stay behind in the care of Mrs Williams from next door.

These visits first made us aware of trains which led on to train-spotting, an activity which for a time came second only to cricket as an all-consuming passion. Standing at the bottom of the garden on a huge mound of earth thrown up by one of Herr Hitler's wayward bombs, and which had by then sprouted a covering of grass which held it together, we watched as Somerset and Dorset trains crossed the bridge over the Lower Bristol Road at the start of the long climb to Combe Down and beyond. The oncoming gradient was so steep that a train of almost any length, either passenger or goods, usually had to be double-headed by two locos and sometimes pushed from behind by a small but willing tank engine into the bargain. You could not help but feel sorry for these lowly drones who pushed from behind, for you knew they would never be free to travel jauntily onwards towards such interesting places as Midsomer Norton, Evercreech Junction, Blandford Forum or even the modest Shoscombe and Middle Hill Halt. From our vantage point we willed each one to make a break for freedom but every time, shortly after the main train had disappeared from view, the dejected tank engine, having pushed with all its might behind the last coach or wagon, would drift backwards to resume its tedious shunting duties in the Green Park sidings, condemned like Sisyphus's stone constantly to reach the crest of the hill, only to roll always back down to the depths of the valley.

There were no such inhibitions for the *Pines Express* whose passing we eagerly awaited as, having fought its way out of the gloom and smog of Birmingham and having refreshed itself in Bath Green Park, it went on its majestic way past the bottom of the garden and on to fashionable, airy Bournemouth. Soon after we had been given our bikes and had been given permission to go outside the estate we discovered that we could rejoin our Somerset and Dorset train friends by cycling to Midford. There we could stand, sit or lie only feet from the tracks and watch most of them thunder past, for very few of them bothered to stop at Midford station. We placed pennies on the lines and tried to retrieve them once the train had passed, hoping to find that they had swelled to huge proportions, or we simply watched as the locomotive executed at speed a manoeuvre which resembled a medieval knight accepting the surrender of a besieged town by taking the keys to the stronghold on the end of his outstretched lance. In this case an iron arm was extended from the loco to grasp a sort of pouch, whose contents were a mystery but which was said to be a foolproof way of ensuring that no two trains could meet on the single track stretch between there and Bath. I never quite fathomed out how it worked.

Photograph by Ivo Peters © Julian Peters

The bridge at the bottom of Brook Road in East Twerton which once carried the Somerset and Dorset Railway over the Lower Bristol Road. In this case the engine seems to have broken free of its carriages or trucks and is making a burst for freedom to Midford.

It was with the *Pines Express* that I first got close up to one of the smoke-belching monsters which roamed the country on uniformed gauged tracks. My grandfather worked for the railway delivering all sorts of goods dropped off by passing trains at Green Park Station where he had many colleagues. One of them was a distant relative whose job was every boy's dream, that of train driver, and not only that, but he regularly drove the *Pines Express* up and down the leg between Birmingham and Bath. The Somerset and Dorset's flagship express would steam majestically into Green

Park which was a dead end. A fresh, fully-rested engine or two would be attached to what had been the back of the train and on the command of a whistle and a green flag waved with a flourish by the guard, the convoy would set off towards the South Coast. Within the train there would be much changing of seats as ladies would have to swap with their men folk since it was not a good thing for feminine metabolism to be travelling with one's back to the engine. Outside, the departed locomotives had left their exhausted, uncoupled comrade looking a little forlorn as it warmed down like a long-distance runner at the buffers at the end of the platform. Once it had regained its breath somewhat the abandoned engine, now bereft of any coaches to pull, would chug sedately and perhaps a trifle light-headedly, still in the hands of the driver and fireman who had brought it all the way from England's second city, back to the sheds, where man and machine would end their shift until the next time.

My grandfather, perhaps noticing in us a burgeoning childhood passion for railways which has never really gone away, particularly in my brother, had arranged as a treat that we would accompany 'Uncle' Ted and his steed on the short journey back to the sheds. My mother, remembering perhaps that my grandfather's last attempt to arrange train travel had resulted in us leaving Bristol for Bath on a train bound for Manchester, necessitating an unscheduled stop to set us down in some ignominy at Mangotsfield, looked on with a certain amount of trepidation as we were hoisted onto the footplate and greeted by the beaming two man crew, one of whose faces was covered in soot, streaked with the sweat which for the last few hours had poured from his brow as he struggled to satisfy the voracious appetite of his coal-eating master. My brother took to it like a duck to water but the roaring fire, the oily smelling plethora of levers and the precarious, draughty work station were too much for me and I wailed to be put back down on the safety of the platform from where I watched my more intrepid brother disappear towards the not too distant sidings. In adulthood he has renewed his acquaintance with the footplate on the Bo'ness Steam Railway near his home in Edinburgh but since this frightening childhood experience I have been content to travel more comfortably but less excitingly in the coaches behind the engine.

This unpromising early close encounter with a steam train did not diminish my fascination with railways. Someone at some stage must have given us an Ian Allan ABC of locomotives, the train-spotter's guides in the form of compendiums which sold for about one and sixpence and which listed all the locomotives with their numbers, and names if applicable, which plied the tracks of a particular region or company or, in the case of the biggest tome, of the whole country. Whenever an engine was 'spotted', its number was neatly underlined, and to see as many as possible became something of an obsession to which thousands of boys became addicted.

In those days train-spotting was mostly a young male person's activity, not the modern comedy club joke which sees it as an indication of some sort of social inadequacy which afflicts a sad throng of uniformly clad middle-aged men. Notebook and pencil in hand we went to any location where trains passed, took down the numbers of locomotives seen and, once back home, underlined with the utmost care those which hitherto had not been spotted. We soon exhausted most of what the Somerset and Dorset could offer and we broadened our horizons to the Great Western with its feudal hierarchy of Kings, Castles, Halls and Granges, and its unnamed tank engines and diesel shunters at the bottom like a caste of untouchables.

Bath Spa was the first serious train-spotting venue. Here for the price of a platform ticket, purchased from a slot machine positioned at the bottom of the stairs leading to the 'Up' platform we could spend all day eagerly awaiting trains going to and coming from all corners of the Great Western Railway. The long distance trains would often slake their thirst from a water fountain at the far end of the 'Down' platform, a long flexible pipe was poked into their boilers like a giant straw. Taking on water was the technical term for this quenching of thirsts and those who were too busy to stop regularly could even do so by scooping up refreshment from troughs placed at intervals in the middle of the tracks. A bit like the ill-mannered action of drinking from the bottle. We learnt the station announcements off by heart: "The train now standing on the 'Up' platform is the …….. for Swindon, calling at Bathampton, Box, Box Mill Lane, Corsham, Chippenham, Christian Malford Halt, Dauntsey, Wootton Bassett and Swindon." Nowadays only Chippenham is deemed worthy of a call. We watched as long convoys of rattling metal cages on wheels carrying mail were dragged by buzzy little electric vehicles from platform to sorting office in nearby Manvers Street and we stood aside deferentially as smartly dressed porters carried ladies' cases up and down the wooden stairs to both platforms, doffing their caps as they were given a little something for their pains. Modern metal trolleys, such as one finds in supermarkets, are hardly a suitable replacement.

From Bath Spa the next logical step in our quest for yet more numbers was Bristol Temple Meads, a few miles to the west, where, from the two extremities of its numerous platforms, we stood a good chance of seeing many more of the locomotives in the GWR's cast list. Moreover, from the highest numbered platforms, in those days on the side nearest the main entrance, we caught sight of slightly different LMS engines, as they trundled to and from distant northern locations such as Manchester, Leeds, Liverpool and even Scotland. This necessitated a new specialist Ian Allan ABC of locomotives. It would not be too many years hence that, at the beginning of each university term, I would be boarding one of these trains which served the northern outposts and clanked its weary way through Britain's industrial heartlands to the North-East, to alight at one of any railway's most impressive backdrops, the majestic soaring structures of Durham City's castle and cathedral. But for a train-spotting boy who had never been further north than the as yet unbuilt M4 corridor such destinations were as remote as Timbuctoo and the baking sands of the Sahara.

Our search for unseen railway engines did once take us south, however. One fine Bank Holiday Monday Chris and I took a special excursion to Bournemouth. Excitedly we joined a host of families toting buckets and spades and other beach paraphernalia and already gorging themselves on bloater paste sandwiches and cherryade. In contrast, apart from some rudimentary items of food and drink, we carried only our notebook and pencil, for we were intent not on building sandcastles and riding donkeys but on getting more numbers to underline in one of Mr Allan's books. By heaving on the heavy leather strap to lower the window in the corridor and leaning out, in spite of notices informing us of the inherent dangers in such an activity, we were able to spot a few locos en route. But it was on the platforms at Bournemouth that we really came into our own, as a series of excursion trains arrived to deposit hundreds of families determined to enjoy a day out at one of Britain's most fashionable resorts. Off they scurried towards the front as we battled our way against the surging flow to get down the number of the instrument of their arrival. The bonus was that many of the trains came from London and other Southern Railway towns and were thus hauled by (to us) exotic green Pacific engines with unfamiliar numbers and names such as Wadebridge, Boscastle and Tangmere. With their trademark side panels they steamed majestically into Bournemouth station like blinkered thoroughbreds on their way to the unsaddling enclosure at the end of a classic race. By late morning all the Bank Holiday specials had arrived, and there was a lull in activity at the station until the early evening when all the trippers had to be transported back to their homes, ready to resume their labours after this brief respite. We did actually wander off to the beach, having taken careful note of the return departure time of the first excursion train, for we did not want to miss any of these exotic, green dragon-like beasts we had perhaps not seen in the morning. On leaving Bournemouth ourselves on our own day-tripping train, along with most other children on board we sank into a satisfied slumber, sated not by sun, sea and sand but by steam and soot from the Southern Pacifics. To encapsulate the wonders of those pre-Beeching days and the hours spent on railway stations the second record has to be *Slow Train* by the incomparable Flanders and Swann.

The best day of the week for us train-spotters in school holidays was Wednesday, for it was then that the GWR works in Swindon were open to the public. It was here that the company's fleet, from the imperious Kings to their lowliest vassals, the humble tank engines, were serviced, cleaned and refurbished. The engines would come in at one end, dirty and dishevelled from the hours of train hauling they had carried out since their last visit to Swindon. On our Wednesday excursions we could follow the progress of these exhausted warriors as they were dismantled and their parts were scrubbed, oiled, repainted and polished. They suffered indignities such as being scoured, purged and re-bored but finally they were reassembled and emerged resplendent from the other end of the shed with their livery restored to its pristine, original state, ready to re-enter the fray of shepherding coaches and trucks around the length and breadth of the GWR network. Engines in various states of undress were still fair game for the assiduous train-spotter but here a moral dilemma was posed: did seeing a small piece of a dismembered locomotive with its number scrawled on it in chalk count as a genuine 'spot'? Purists undoubtedly said no but we pragmatists would take anything we could get and on returning home the underlining took place, not without a pang of conscience perhaps.

In spite of roaming the streets of Odd Down, on foot or on bikes, or of journeying further afield in search of the numbers and names fixed to railway locomotives, the principal theatre of our activities remained 'the Players', the truncated residue of the pre-war Odd Down Playing Fields. The area was still big enough to house four or five football pitches, three hockey pitches, a couple of rugby areas at the bottom and several cricket squares. For a short while there was even provision for polo on bicycles, a plebeian version of an otherwise inaccessible aristocratic game, which did not really ever catch on. The fact that both sides after a short while seemed inevitably to end up in a tangled heap of flailing pedals, aimlessly spinning wheels and punctured tyres probably hastened the demise of what was the closest Odd Down could come to extreme sports in the 50s.

Dotted around the perimeter were dark brown, creosoted, and thus rather evil-smelling sheds in which participants in proper matches could change. No showers and toilets, of course, just a few pegs around the walls and a rough wooden floor which embedded long splinters into the feet of unsuspecting sportsmen, thus incapacitating some of them before they even started. The main operating tool of the St John's Ambulance man present on match days was a pair of tweezers. To differentiate these brown hutches one from another, a large number was painted on the front of each one in glittering white. On match days a board at the entrance to the fields would direct the gladiators to their preparation area and their field of conflict. Thus

it might proclaim: Bath Cabinet Makers v Stothert and Pitt 2,3. This was not a forecast of the score but meant that the teams, comprised in this case of workers who made furniture for post-war homes or cranes to be found in every port in the world, knew where to change and where they would be playing. Spectators too, usually three or four of us boys and an errant dog who had to be constantly dissuaded from joining in the pursuit of the ball, were informed of the venue of the encounter.

The Lone Ranger in the back garden of the prefab. In the background is Maggs's cottage, home to the siren Ann, which still stands in Bloomfield Road. To the right of the stone house stands one of the creosoted brown shacks which served as changing rooms over 'the Players'.

There were often a few more people watching the rugby exchanges at the bottom of the field, but we were rarely attracted by this violent, steaming spectacle. Hockey too failed to excite us, a whirling stop-start short activity in which even girls could take part. In those days it was football matches in winter and cricket in summer which monopolised all our attention as spectators.

On match days we could only watch while our elders indulged their sporting fantasies but at all other times, whether 'the Players' were officially open or not, the area became our own playground and sports arena. That is, as long as the world's greatest spoilsport, Burfy, did not get in the way.

George Burford was the groundsman who looked after 'the Players'. He was particularly fussy about the pitches and squares which he tended with great care. Unfortunately he viewed the unofficial use of them by young boys to be as damaging as any weed or fungus known to Man. He didn't seem to mind if we played out our test matches and cup finals around the less well groomed periphery of his domain but encroachment on the hallowed playing areas incurred his constant wrath. Hockey goals were particularly attractive to diminutive footballers as their smaller size made them ideal for goalmouth scrambles. Fortunately for us, but certainly not for him, Burfy was lame and on foot he was no match for youthful legs and so, if we encroached on forbidden territory, he would hunt us down on his motor mower. And so, for most of our impromptu games, we would post a look-out and, as soon as the deranged Burfy was spotted bearing down on us at full throttle on his Atco Thunderer, up would go the cry "Watch out! 'Ere comes Burfy." Coats were grabbed, balls were stuck under arms, stumps were wrenched from the ground, a bit in the modern manner of test players taking them as trophies of victory, and we legged it as fast as we could over Maggs's wall and into the sanctuary of our garden, leaving our tormentor fuming – but satisfied that the state of his precious pitches had been preserved.

Our games of cricket were left largely unscathed since, out of choice, we sited them right up against the tall wire fence in front of the prefab gardens. This obviated the need for a wicket-keeper, for whom we had no equipment, and any fielders behind the bat. Fielders were often a scarce commodity. When I was first allowed to join in with the big boys I was uniquely deployed as a fielder and, with these beginnings, I should, in later life, have turned into a Colin Bland or a Derek Randall but this metamorphosis never took place. After a bit, when slightly older arms got tired, I was allowed to bowl. Easy pickings they probably thought. To begin with I almost certainly did serve up some cannon fodder but I soon learnt that it was fatal to send down a) long-hops and b) even worse, anything on or outside the leg stump, since this was immediately dispatched with most of my fellow practitioners' one shot, a lusty heave to leg. I discovered that, if I pitched it up and kept it on the off side, no contact was usually made and the ball thudded into the wire-meshed fence. Such tactics were condemned by frustrated, one-shot batsmen as a form of cheating on a par with throwing. "Bowl properly" was the usual gripe.

A few years later, when I started to receive coaching at Hampset, I was advised by Rosey "to pitch it a foot outside the off stump and make the batsman come to you" and I had no problems with this, as I'd been doing it for ages, as a way of avoiding having to go miles to retrieve the ball since the philosophy of "you bowled it, you fetch it" was often invoked at 'the Players', whenever a particularly long trek was involved. Rosey did not have a great deal of success when trying to coach us. He once spent all week before an encounter with local rivals Fairway telling us how to counter the wiles of Ken Cole, a bowler who did nothing with the ball but bowled to an immaculate length, posted a deep mid-on and mid-off and waited for the batsman to tire in the war of attrition. We thought we took all his warnings on board. On the following Saturday K Cole took all ten wickets. I thought at the time how nice it would be to do the same. I couldn't rely, however, on the rash intemperance of a series of youths to do it for me. Rosey's advice on bowling was by no means infallible for I soon began to bowl against more than one-shot wonders who rather unsportingly went onto the back foot and, unless the ball was pitched right up in the block-hole, smashed it through the off side, an area which at 'the Players' one could safely leave totally unprotected.. A radical re-think became necessary and Ken Saunders' more conservative advice provided the answer: "Pitch it on or fractionally outside the off stump and turn it, quickly if possible, about half the width of the bat." No such sophistication was ever required over 'the Players' but at least I had learnt there to avoid straying down the leg side too much.

Occasionally, towards the end of a cricketing session in Burfy's domain, some slightly older conscience would be pricked and someone would concede that "we ought to let Malc have a bat." Objections were almost certainly raised, "'E'll get 'urt", "'E's too small, the bat's too big", "'E's 'ad a good bowl". In spite of these I did sometimes make it to the crease, but after two or three balls it was unanimously agreed that it was time for tea or looked like rain or someone's Mum wanted errands to be run and the game would come to an end. "You can bat first next time," was always offered as a sop but the promise was never kept. No wonder I never blossomed as a batsman, but perhaps that was a blessing in disguise.

For several years Burfy was thus a hate figure, the destroyer of young talent, a kill-joy and a spoil sport in the most literal of ways. It was only later, when I started to frequent Hampset, that I realised that our early antipathy to the long-suffering groundsman was misplaced. George lived in a terraced house on Bloomfield Road just above the Crescent, and his garden almost backed onto the cricket club. At weekends he would quite often come to watch the final stages of matches in what must have been a real busman's holiday for him. Towards the end of the game he would enjoy a glass of stout before limping the short way back home. I soon discovered that George was a softly-spoken, kind and sensitive person, he was said to be an accomplished musician and a widely-read man, all of which did not fit the monstrous picture we had erroneously built up of him. His motorised pursuit of us as we hacked his pitches to pieces was born only of pride and not from an obsessive desire to deny pleasure to all sporting children.

'The Players' were thus the arena where, in spite of Burfy's best efforts, we developed our sporting skills and on one occasion it became the site of an exciting real life drama. One fine Friday evening a bright yellow bi-plane came circling over our playground. 'Rosey and the Tiger Moth' sounds like an episode from a Tintin adventure, for it was rumoured that the plane tried at first to land at Hampset and that 'Rosey', no doubt recalling the early spotter planes from his youthful days on the Somme, with an imperious wave of his groundsman's fork, sent the errant contraption in the direction of 'the Players', in order to preserve the square he so carefully tended. Of all pieces of folklore this must be one of the most apocryphal, for even this, as it turned out, incompetent would not have tried to alight on an area as small as Hampset. Out as usual on our bikes around the streets of the estate, we were aware of the Tiger Moth circling our domain. This was definitely Biggles and/or Ginger on a secret mission or even Saint-Exupéry, miraculously restored from the dead, who had come to play out an exciting drama on Odd Down. The bi-plane lurched its way over Noad's Corner taking with it a chimney stack and a recently erected TV aerial from a house in Frome Road and sank slowly over 'the Players', coming to a juddering halt somewhere near the bottom, after having gouged a couple of deep furrows out of Burfy's pitches and squares, thus literally in one fell swoop doing more damage than we had ever managed with our impromptu matches.

It took a few moments for the significance of the event to sink in but then, along with most of the youth of Odd Down, it seemed, we were off on our bikes, pedalling furiously across Burfy's pitches to offer assistance to the exotic creature who had so unexpectedly arrived amongst us. The police, however, had beaten us to it; they had already thrown a cordon around the aircraft, had posted a guard and were leading away a rather shamefaced, leather-jacketed, goggle-wearing figure. This was proof positive that international espionage, gun-running or, at the very least, smuggling was involved, Saturday morning pictures brought to reality in the most unlikely of spots.

Alas the explanation was much more disappointingly prosaic. *The Bath and Wilts Chronicle and Herald*, to give it its full title, informed us the next evening that the intrepid aviator was merely an incompetent who had got hopelessly lost and had run out of fuel. On Monday morning, having been resupplied with whatever drove his Tiger Moth, he took off again, his tail between his legs, no doubt having been given a new map and precise instructions on how to get home to his mum. Burfy's thoughts on the matter were never, to my knowledge, recorded.

To remember this strange episode, when I am marooned on my desert island and perhaps in the hope that a similar errant Tiger Moth might appear from nowhere to rescue me, I think I'll have Frank Sinatra and *Come fly with me* as record number three.

Education, Education, Education

My early years on Odd Down were thus given over to pure hedonism, slightly impoverished pleasure-seeking, but hedonism nonetheless with days spent outdoors in endless physical activity or indoors, when the weather was inclement, in more sedate pastimes. There came a time, however, when the need to go to school arose. Learning to read from the sides of buses and other vehicles was not going to suffice.

Before any first experience of formal education, however, it was just me, a few friends of my age, Mike Hillman to the fore, and my patient, hat-wearing-at-all-times mother. I do not know where and when I acquired my adult, profound aversion to shopping but it was certainly not in these earliest days, for I loved going to the shops. We rarely required much in the way of groceries, because my father brought most of what we needed home from work at the Co-op. If we did run short of anything essential, the first port of call was Sly's, one of two contiguous shops on the top road. The right-hand one was run by Mrs Singer. I assume there was a Mr Singer but he never appeared in the shop; he was probably out doing other work, leaving the retail outlet to his wife. We did not often patronise her establishment, not out of any animosity towards the good lady, but because Mr Sly – it never struck me how inappropriate his name was for customer relations – had a better selection, particularly of sweets. Our entry into his emporium was announced by a jingly-jangly bell and, when this sounded, Mr Sly would emerge silently through a sort of curtain made up of coloured strips of plastic, with an enquiring look of weary servitude on his face. He was a somewhat diminutive man with slicked back dark hair. He broke with the tradition of the lower echelons of public servants, who always wore a long brown cotton working coat, by favouring the same garment but in bluey grey. The top pocket of his coat was studded by a row of coloured pens which seemed totally redundant because, if there was ever any need to do a calculation, he took a thickly leaded pencil from behind his ear which needed a lick to make it function. Dispensing quarters of loose sweets was done with an experienced flourish, allowing the precious items to be filtered through waggling fingers until the exact amount in weight had been released from the big glass jar into the silver receptacle of his scales from where the contents were deftly poured into a small white bag the two corners of which were held between the thumb and first finger of each hand and the sweets were swung in a few circles to form a temporary seal. A few seconds only elapsed from the start to the end of this complicated manœuvre. Sly's was the first shop I was allowed to visit on my own, always with an instruction to 'mind the road' and, in the earliest times, clutching treasured sweet ration coupons.

Just beyond the two grocers on the top road was Archie Bridges, not a shop, merely the front room of one of the houses where the said Archie cut most of the male hair on Odd Down. Archie was an old fashioned barber, not a new-fangled hairdresser, for his expertise did not go beyond a rudimentary short back and sides. Children were shorn particularly short; there was never any chance of hair getting in one's eyes. My mother was a little sceptical about Archie's credentials and, when we were a bit older, tried to take us to Swifts in Moorland Road, which was usually populated by middle-aged ladies sitting under a strange hollow contraption while they waited for something to happen to their hair, or even to a place in town which had two separate sections for the two sexes and where they offered to squirt an oily liquid on your hair and even held up a mirror behind your head seeking your approval when they had finished their operations. As if we would have had either the courage or the expertise to complain! But for all this sophistication I preferred a scalping at Archie's hands because he had one topic of conversation – sport. He did not share his horse-racing tips and his thoughts on every sport under the sun with small boys but, if you had to wait while he finished off an adult, you could eavesdrop on what at first seemed highly informed rhetoric but which, once we gained some discernment, was pure prejudice. At least it was entertaining, and getting one's haircut is rarely an entertaining activity.

It was also a great pleasure to go or be sent to get fresh bread from Noad's. Locals in the know soon learnt when Mr Noad's baking times were. When the shop at the front of the bakery was shut you could always go to the side door to get a loaf straight from the oven. Because of the heat, the door was virtually always open and through it in the gloom of the interior you could make out a floured spectral figure flitting to and fro in the frenetic creation of the staff of life. "Can I have a large white please?" would put a temporary halt to this ghostly bustle and Mr Noad the baker, sounding just like a member of one of the Happy Families we sometimes played with, would proffer one of the objects he had just brought into the world in exchange for a penny or two. On the short walk home little fingers could be poked far into the warm interior of the loaf to extract a doughy foretaste of the bread to come, with the result that, when sliced a little later for teatime bread and jam, each piece bore the telltale signs of this clandestine extraction in the shape of neat holes which made the bread look like a piece of foreign cheese which we had only seen in pictures.

The most exciting shop, however, was the Odd Down Co-op, which in those times consisted of two separate establishments side by side. To the left was the butcher's, all marble slabs, tiled floors covered in sawdust and metal hooks from which hung pieces of dead animal in all shapes and sizes waiting to be hacked, chopped, minced or sawed up to order. To the right stood the grocery. Customers were served here in different departments: dairy, dried goods, fruit and veg etc. There was certainly as yet no question of wandering around, transatlantic style, helping oneself from a series of shelves or fixtures, as they somewhat strangely soon came to be known. Once the goods were assembled, the price to be paid calculated and the money handed over, the bill and the wherewithal to settle it were encased in a long cylinder and sent zooming skywards like a motorised trapeze artist on a complicated network of pulleys and wires to a cashier perched high in a solitary eyrie, who dealt with the transaction and sent the change and the 'divvy' slip back along the same tortuous mechanical web, the workings of which were a constant source of wonder and amazement to young eyes. The 'divvy' slips were most important for, at the end of every quarter or half year

46

Co-op membership would yield its rewards, a proportion of all that had been spent in the period would be calculated and returned as one's dividend. The little slips were the only way to keep tabs on how much was due.

Every week my mother carefully 'did her tins' on pay day, inserting into a series of tins an allotted amount for milk, coal, clothes, insurance and so forth and when the' divvy' date came round extra time was given over to this meticulous husbandry, the totals being carefully recorded in a small exercise book. When I was eventually allowed to run errands on my own, I was always given strict instructions to make sure they took down the 'divvy' number, 5489 (my mother's number) or 4258, if an errand was run on behalf of Aunty Floss. These figures are etched for ever onto my mind. "What's your number, love?" the assistant would ask. "5489" and the amount spent would be written onto a block of perforated tickets, separated by blue carbon paper. The top copy went home and the bottom part to the Co-op offices for the due dividend to be worked out. For milk and bread the Co-op did not deal in money at all but in tokens made of some very inferior metal, making them look like coinage of some tin-pot eastern state.

Sometimes we ventured into town on the no. 11 bus and the destination was usually again the Co-op at its Westgate Buildings headquarters. Non-grocery items here qualified not only for the precious 'divvy' but also for staff discount. By modern standards I suppose that this was not a particularly large building but it was substantial and imposing enough to house a lift, the only one I encountered in my formative years. What is more it even had a man whose sole purpose in life was to operate this modern marvel, which my mother was a little reluctant to enter in the belief that it was bound sooner or later to break down with us trapped inside it. The operative was a dapper man who wore the usual ubiquitous brown coat but his slight superiority in rank, real or imagined, was signalled by two green velvet stripes on his lapels and the letters CWS emblazoned in gold across his breast pocket. Having been warily, in my mother's case, summoned by the large button which I was allowed to press, he would open from within the sturdy double defences in the shape of a sliding door and a grill-like gate and solemnly announce if he was ascending or descending. He was acquainted with my mother and showed her great deference as she was an ex-office worker from the hallowed third floor which was out of bounds to the public. He would, however, on request, take my mother and me up to this lofty sanctum so that she could renew acquaintance with the 'girls in the office'. Each year Christmas cards would arrive simply inscribed 'With season's greetings' from Joan or Ethel or Winifred. On enquiry about the originator of these festive thoughts we were told that the said person was a 'girl from the office'. I regularly met these ladies, either in Westgate Buildings or sometimes in the street in Bath and, if wearing one, I was enjoined to doff my cap to them. I tried to assume a suitable air of gallantry but it always struck me, on encountering one of these venerable, soberly clad ladies, that by no stretch of the imagination, could they be described as 'girls', at least not from what I understood of the term, in fact they appeared to be very ancient examples of the female species.

In my earliest days I imagined that ushering people up and down in the lift to haberdashery, china and glass or soft furnishings and then escorting them back to street level with their neatly wrapped purchases must have been a rewarding and exciting way to spend one's time, but in retrospect I realise that it must have been unutterably tedious. One day we found the operative absent from his post and the lift unmanned. "Cut-backs," announced my mother frostily and, in the absence of the deferential servant, we had to push the buttons ourselves. Button number three had been covered in heavy masking tape, our laissez-passer to the nerve centre of the Co-op's activities had been removed with the demise of the ageing bell-hop. In his memory please, Ms Young, record number 4 must be Tommy Steele's *Elevator Rock*, the B side to one of the first vinyl 45s I ever bought.

I rarely recall shopping with my father. After spending all week slicing bacon, cutting cheese and weighing out loose tea he was probably loth to spend any of his precious spare time on the receiving end of shopping. The only purchasing expeditions we engaged in were to get leather with which to mend our shoes.

Sgt. Kenneth Charles Johnson, ex Bath Co-op, photographed just before helping to bowl a few unplayable deliveries to a German side captained by Herr Rommel on a sandy wicket in North Africa.

Back in civvy street Sgt. Johnson finds it impossible not to 'stand at ease' in front of the camera. Younger son adopts a similar, military pose. Note the belt with its S shaped clasp which at the time held up virtually all youthful trousers, whether long or short.

My father, like so many combatants, did not talk about the war to any great extent but from snatches of conversation here and there we managed to piece together his experiences. After dealing with North Africa he and his mates proceeded to Italy but about half way up the boot he was lightly injured in the foot. Unfortunately the ambulance taking him to be patched up, either through driving incompetence or as a result of coming under fire, ended up in an Italian ditch. The person next to him was killed and my father sustained a very serious back injury which for the rest of his life necessitated the wearing of a strange corset-like garment into which he had to be tightly strapped.

With his experience at the Bath Co-op Sgt. Johnson is the obvious man to oversee the provision of essential supplies during the push up through Italy. The crates are mostly marked 'Birra Peroni Roma' but the bottles look more like Corona Dandelion and Burdock. Certainly they do not look much like Peroni Nastro Azzurro which is now marketed as a rather sophisticated beverage.

Somewhere along the line he also contracted malaria which returned periodically to cause profuse perspiring and shaking. During these bouts the sweat was often said to be so severe that 'it came through onto the floor.' His injuries and indisposition brought about, firstly, evacuation to Capri and, later, repatriation and lengthy convalescence in the less romantic surroundings of Chertsey. In compensation he received a disability pension of a few shillings a week, but I'm sure he would gladly have relinquished this in exchange for a loss of back pain and the regular bouts of sweating.

Whilst at Chertsey, presumably to alleviate the tedium, he learnt, amongst other things, to mend shoes and so, when anyone's soles wore thin, an expedition to procure leather was called for. Half-way up Broad Street, obtusely one of the narrower streets in Bath, on the right, more or less opposite to where, in a few years' time, I would go to Secondary School, before King Edward's moved out of the city centre, was a shop which sold leather off-cuts. It has long since disappeared, demolished to make way for a road improvement scheme but it must have been a saddlery or some such business and it exuded the most wonderful smell of leather, a smell which has remained with me for ever and has meant that the only fashion shop I can now enter with any feeling remotely like pleasure is one which sells good quality handbags. When we entered the Broad Street home of leather the proprietor would appear, clad of course in the uniform brown coat, descending a few steps from some back work space. From a large container he would offer squares and rectangles in various sizes of delightfully smelling light tan material. There would ensue much bending and flexing of these pieces until my father was satisfied both with the size and the quality of the article. It would then be taken home and with the help of a strange, three-footed metal object would be transferred to the soles of the shoes needing refurbishment, secured by a series of wickedly pointed tacks and pared to the correct shape with an extremely sharp knife which I was enjoined never to touch. At least we were well shod.

Quite a number of vendors came to the house. The Co-op would, if required, deliver milk and bread in exchange for their own currency of inferior metal discs. Long before the advent of on-line grocery shopping a man would call, take an order and, later in the week, a box of groceries would appear. There were less frequent arrivals too. Occasionally an archetypal French onion seller appeared on an ancient black bicycle, but his wares were always politely refused.

Once a year, around Christmas time a representative of Showerings of Shepton Mallet called to enquire if we needed any seasonal wine, Christmas being the only time such imbibing was remotely contemplated. My mother was firmly of the opinion that a glass of Burgundy at this time did wonders for one's health but never explained why its medicinal qualities were ineffective at other times of the year. These visits ceased once a sparkling perry drink in small blue bottles, which featured a yellow Bambi-type creature, had made the company millions in spite of the fact that the French successfully got them banned from including the word champagne in the description of the fizzy phenomenon. This drink also got the maternal seal of approval at Christmas, and she insisted on pronouncing its final syllable as it was written, 'Babycham', and not with a 'sh' sound, undermining the suggestion of counterfeiting to which the French were trying to object. The parent company was no longer interested in supplying the small amounts of drink we and our, of necessity, abstemious neighbours were likely to purchase.

Ice-cream sellers, accompanied by discordant musical chimes made regular appearances, and one enterprising purveyor of summer ices turned his van in winter into a mobile source of faggots and peas. On hearing the familiar clarion call on a winter's evening when it was already dark and chill, one issued forth with a large earthenware basin into which was dollopped a generous portion of glutinous comfort food which had a distinctive odour and which, as I recall, was very tasty. The one drawback to this particular fast food was that it induced a considerable amount of flatulence in all those who consumed it.

Some callers were not as welcome and, if they came knocking at the door, one had to pretend not to be in, as long as their impending arrival had been well spotted in advance. The first such group were gypsies. If these people were seen on the top road heading in our direction and carrying baskets of their staple wares, heather and wooden clothes pegs, I was ushered in quickly, if I was not already in the house, and told to hide under the table. There we stayed silently holding our breath until they had knocked several times and gone away. But still we could not leave our hideaway for these cunning itinerants would sometimes go round the back and catch us red-handed in our attempts to shun them. The purpose of this subterfuge was to avoid having to buy any of the gypsies' unwanted goods, because my mother was convinced that, if you refused outright what they had to offer, they would, in their resentment, impose some sort of curse on you which brought bad luck infinitely worse even than that brought by breaking a mirror or walking under a ladder.

A couple of years ago I had to go to a school in Kent to give some insight into the exam system. At Charing Cross, when I asked for a day return to my destination in Kent with the appropriate Senior Railcard reduction, the ticket vendor, a young man with a London accent and a resplendent green turban, opined that I must be an impostor, as I could not possibly be old enough to qualify for the said card. I wondered immediately if this pleasant young man exchanging such good-humoured, flattering banter with railway customers could be the son or grandson of one of the second group of people whose appearance also sent us diving for cover under the table. For a short period, probably before they acquired corner shops, restaurants and other businesses, the no. 11 bus would occasionally disgorge onto Odd Down pavements a small group of tall, dark-skinned, turban-wearing exotic creatures toting heavy suitcases which contained silk garments such as ties and scarves which they attempted to sell door-to-door. On catching sight of them in the distance my mother would at once order us into the familiar under-the-table retreat – not because of any racist feelings, I don't think she would have understood such a concept, but simply because she was frightened of these strange people, the like of which she had never seen before.

Soon my mother had to take refuge under the furniture alone on seeing the people who provoked such fear in her for I had to go to school. In the September after my fifth birthday I joined the ranks of St Luke's Primary School. The first day did not prove to be a great start. I spent the morning happily doing whatever activities had been devised for the new arrivals by the wife of the headmaster Mr H.W.G. Smart, consumed my packed lunch and then was told I had to go to bed for a rest. No namby-pamby just going for half days for a term to get used to school life, we were plunged straight into full sessions but, because of their length, it was deemed necessary for the very youngest to have a post-prandial siesta. I suppose if it was good enough for Winston Churchill it was good enough for us but I considered it a complete waste of time. What was the point of coming to school to go to bed? You might as well be at home listening to *Workers' Playtime*. They might have on Cyril Fletcher, the Clitheroe Kid, Archie Andrews or, my favourite, Stanley Unwin who talked gobbledegook which somehow made sense. So I slipped out of the makeshift dormitory and made my way home, up the road past Telford's paper shop (son Alan was to become a great Hampset stalwart), past Littler's butcher's, left at the Chapel at

Noad's Corner (now a furniture repository of some description) and over the main road to home. My mother was amazed to see me, "What are you doing here?" "They tried to put me to bed." Sensibly she took me straight back. I still saw no point in enforced slumber and so a compromise was reached: I was to be allowed to read or draw while my classmates snoozed contentedly.

I enjoyed school after that inauspicious start. For the first time we engaged in organised games, particularly football on a postage stamp sized pitch just below the school in Rush Hill, and we even played matches against other schools usually on a Saturday morning. Mr Frisby was our coach, or at least he blew his whistle from time to time. He would appear struggling up the hill from his home somewhere in the Southdown area, our strip, recently laundered by his wife in her new twin tub, contained in a carrier bag attached to the handlebars of his ancient boneshaker. The coveted blue shirts with gold numbers, mine was no. 10, Nicky Smith 9 and Mike Bissex 8, were handed out. We played a classic W formation, no 4-4-2 or other weird combination, though actually we probably adopted the classic primary school tactic of simply all chasing the ball around wherever it went, which from time to time was out into Rush Hill and under an unsuspecting vehicle. The one shirt I was glad not to have to don was the goalkeeper's no. 1. Like all other goalies' jerseys of the time it was a prickly green affair with a high round collar, rougher on the skin than the hair shirt of any medieval penitent. Everyone was delighted to cede the privilege of wearing this hideous garment to Bob Staunton and after him Ron White, both later to become long-serving Hampset figures. The former was so disfigured by the experience of wearing such an encumbrance that a bit further on in his sporting career he took up rugby. I doubt if we won very often but that was not the point; the thrill of playing as a member of a team had been tasted and found to be worth pursuing. I even got to write the match accounts to be read out in assembly for which task I adopted the sensational style of the *News of the World*'s sports pages which we devoured every Sunday.

Academic matters were not ignored, either. The redoubtable Misses Barber and Brown, who lived in the misplaced-on-the-wrong-hill Bloomfield Crescent, were in charge of the top classes and with them we were schooled in the mysteries of how to pass the 11-plus. The approach was of course entirely didactic; we sat in serried ranks at wooden desks and were told what to do. Writing was performed with a nibbed pen, replenished from time to time with ink from a porcelain ink well let into a specially customised hole on the desk. We parsed sentences, completed grammar exercises and wrote stories. We also made essential calculations such as determining how long it would take to fill baths given the capacity of the tub and the rate of flow from the taps and, my favourite, where two trains would cross given the times they left Paddington and Bristol and their respective average rates of progress. I must have got rather good at most of this pointless training because I passed and got a scholarship to go to King Edward's where I could join my brother but had to say goodbye to most of my school and, by now, Hampset pals.

High days and holidays

Changing from Primary to Secondary School coincided, just about, with the first time we went on holiday – holiday, that is, in the sense of staying away from home in a different place. A colleague of my father owned a caravan which was parked at Berrow on the Bristol Channel Coast and he offered it to us for a week. Not only that, he was also willing to drive us there and back in a large but somewhat battered Austin which he possessed. It all seemed to be too good to be true but there were two flies in the ointment – our brace of cats. They had never been in a cattery before, and a neighbour's prized moggy had returned from such an establishment traumatised and full of fleas, so there was no question of our 'Life of Reilly' cats being boarded out. Our first holiday seemed scuppered before it began, but then our resourceful and stoical mother came to the rescue; she would travel back and forth each day.

This solution having been found, off we went sunk deep in the back-seat tattered luxury of the black (there were no other colours for cars then) Austin. The males of the family were installed in the caravan, and my mother went back home with the Good Samaritan chauffeur. On every weekday of the following week, there was no possibility of undertaking the trip relying on the Sunday service, she made the journey from Odd Down to Berrow by public transport, a complicated itinerary involving two or three changes at various bus stations. She would arrive late morning, spend a few hours with us, tidy up the caravan, prepare an early tea, my father was a dab hand at breakfasts but did not cook much else, and then retrace her bus steps to get back home in the evening 'to see to the cats'. The two felines thrived on such pampering, for they both lived to a great age and at the time they almost certainly purred out their gratitude. With the insouciance of youth we probably took this self-sacrifice on my mother's part for granted and got on with extracting the maximum amount of pleasure from our week on the coast, before our limousine returned on the second Saturday to take us home in regal style. In those days there were only a very few caravans resident on Brean Down, and we had the long expanse of beach and dunes largely to ourselves. The weather was fine but breezy, conditions which played havoc with my hair-do. Just prior to coming away I had been scalped on a visit to Archie Bridges and during the holiday week the keen breeze coming off the Bristol Channel drove the remains of my locks into stiff peaks in the middle of my skull, giving me the appearance of a spiky Mohican long before punks were ever dreamed of.

Apart from this proper holiday, we indulged in nothing other than day trips, excursions usually by train to one of the two Ws, Weston-super-Mare in one direction and Weymouth in the other. These might take place in my father's two weeks' holiday from work or else, because he worked a six-day week (half-day closing Thursdays) at the Co-op, on a summer or early autumn Sunday. Since the Sunday special inevitably departed well before any Bristol Omnibus interrupted its sabbath lie-in to labour up the hill to Odd Down, our outings always began with a walk to Bath Spa station, quite a walk for little legs but at least it was all down hill. We also had quite a bit to carry, buckets, spades, bats, balls, lemonade and sandwiches – any combination of egg, cheese or ham. Whilst the food was being prepared we waited impatiently outside in the early morning air; if we had strayed far into September the spiders may well have cast their ghostly webs across the privet hedge at the front of the house. Then it was off bearing our day trip impedimenta down the hill, over the Bear Flat, across the Old Bridge to the station. We obviously returned in time to catch the last Sunday evening bus, because fortunately I can never recall having to trudge back up the hill after an exhausting day at the seaside.

Non-corridor trains had just about been phased out but a lack of rolling stock sometimes saw them pressed back into service for one-off excursions. Acquaintance with these convoys from which there was no chance of escape whilst moving has bred in me the need to go for a pee before any train journey, however short or luxurious. Mostly we were blessed with corridor trains, composed of compartments for about eight people and wonderful string-netted shelves above head height for luggage, and with side corridors, a godsend for small boys with untrained bladders, weakened by lemonade. Whichever W was the destination for the day, we always had to gather in the centre of the platform in the hope that we would be able to find seats in the middle of the train, the part deemed less vulnerable in the collisions which my mother believed were likely to happen to all trains. To this day I still find it odd to sit in the coaches at the extreme ends of any train, a pity since this is often where the newly designated quiet zones are to be found, the last refuge from whining music players and inane telephone conversations – though even this refuge is not always respected.

Weymouth was probably the better resort, certainly as far as going in the sea was concerned and for facilities in general: fish and chips, candy floss, toffee apples and kiss-me-quick cowboy hats. But for beach cricket Weston was better, since the tide was virtually never in and there were wide expanses of a mixture of sand and mud which under the sun's rays usually provided a more durable wicket than the finer South Coast sand, something akin to what we might experience on the sub-continent if we ever got that far to play. On arriving on the promenade all others expressed disappointment if the sea was not in, but we were delighted at the prospect of a belter of a beach wicket. The only trouble with going to Weston was that beach activities usually started quite late, the delay being caused by my maternal grandfather who, particularly after he became a widower when I was about five years old, often accompanied us on our excursions. He was an ex-drayman and deliverer of goods sent by rail, originally plying his trade with a horse and cart. This employment had developed in him a professional interest in, and a penchant for, beer. Any beer was palatable but it happened that a certain elixir known by the initials M and B was deemed to have unsurpassable qualities. It so happened that between Weston-super-Mare train station and the sea front was a public house which dispensed this life-giving liquid and on arrival in the resort granddad could not possibly give up the opportunity to indulge in a couple of pints of it and, if Uncle Fred was part of the expedition, this increased to at least four or five. Whilst this whistle wetting was going on we were left in the beer garden with mother and aunty, if she was with us, and the traditional lemonade and a packet of crisps – Smith's, of course, with the trademark little blue bag of salt. My father was constantly encouraged not to keep up with the other two in sinking pints because, as he was reminded, "you can't take it like those two." He must have taken the advice because he was never unable to take his turn at bowling when we eventually made it to the beach. The delay was annoying because all the best pitches had already been claimed by more abstemious day trippers, but at least the rear side of granddad, ensconced in a deck chair and enjoying post M and B slumber, provided a suitable wicket.

Even on the beach I cannot recall batting much, bowling yes and even more fielding, dodging family groups on the sands, mumbling apologies to grannies whose hat had been disturbed by a well struck cover drive, avoiding meandering donkeys and large pools of water left behind by the sea which had long since disappeared out of sight towards the distant Welsh coast. At least the absence of the sea and any possibility of paddling or bathing meant that there were fewer alternatives to beach test matches. When play was curtailed, perhaps by the arrival of a few clouds or even some spots of rain, but most likely because of fatigue, the pier usually merited a visit before our return to the station. Fatigue probably ensured that we availed ourselves of the possibility of travelling the length of the pier, one way at least, on a little brightly coloured jaunty train. But only one way because we didn't want to miss out on the penny slot machines which ran down the middle of the walkway to tempt the more energetic promenaders. At the end of the pier was to be found the more serious entertainment: bingo, a crazy house, the hall of mirrors, a helter-skelter and the horrors of the ghost train. Ever since I had won a plaster of Paris 'Home Sweet Home' dog at the fair on Odd Down, which still sits proudly on grandma's old piano in our front room some sixty years later, I particularly liked to fish out plastic yellow ducks which swam around in a never-ending circle and which bore a number on their underbelly. The total of the three numbers on the ducks you were allowed to hook might lead to a prize, but it rarely seemed to.

Beach cricket at Weymouth was more difficult. The more crowded beach and the shifting finer sand militated against it, and the preferred activities became sorties in smartly painted pedalo craft or sand sculpture in which we tried to emulate the marvellous structures created by a gentleman who had a permanent pitch at one end of the beach and who presumably existed on the pennies thrown by holidaymakers amazed at the scale and realism of his creations. Weymouth at the time was altogether smarter, perhaps that is hard to believe now, the demise of the English seaside resort having wreaked its havoc, and it was always a thrill to walk the short distance from the station and take in the splendid sight of the Regency promenade and the impressive clock. Securing deckchairs here and knowing when to move on before the attendant arrived to exact his dues was an art in itself.

Slightly more complicated day trips could be attempted by boat. The ships in question were the paddle steamers belonging to Campbell's White Funnel Fleet which crisscrossed the Bristol Channel, calling at a series of ports and resorts on either side. It was not quite the Mississippi but for several years, until the ever increasing spread of the motor car and the eventual construction of a road bridge scuppered them, these delightful craft brought us fun and adventure. What's more the bracing air of the Bristol Channel was good for us, at least in my mother's eyes. Once in mid-channel we were invariably exhorted to take deep breaths and lungfuls of this free and invigorating commodity. On days on which a White Funnel Fleet excursion had been decided upon, an early start took us into town and a second bus whisked us off to Hotwells in Bristol to embark on our steamer, perhaps *The Bristol Queen* or its Welsh sister *The Cardiff Queen,* for both of the major cities on each side had a boat regally named after them. Usually our destination was somewhere in South Wales but occasionally we went to Clevedon or Ilfracombe on 'our' side of the Channel. There were several possible disembarkation locations on the South Wales coast. The only one I can recall with any clarity is Barry Island to whose gaudy attractions we were exposed long before *Gavin and Stacey* brought them more universal exposure. In particular we thrilled at the helter-skelter which was so much higher and steeper than the one on the end of Weston pier.

The Bristol Queen

It must have been about the same time that we became aware of music. As teenagers in the Sixties I suppose the English pop music scene should have made the most impact on us, but we had already been spoken for as far as music was concerned. I do remember on a couple of occasions going to 'concerts' at the Bath Pavilion at which sixties pop groups aroused a great deal of screaming from young female inhabitants. Of those seen live The Searchers and The Hollies were the only ones which made any lasting impression, the former in particular for a rousing rendition of *Needles and Pins.* I think I'm right in saying that the Beatles never played in Bath, but they used a city hotel, I believe it was the Francis, to stop-over after a performance in Bristol and when this became common knowledge there was much shinning up drainpipes and resorting to other ingenious methods of entry in order to get a glimpse of the Fab Four. I can't imagine their fellow guests were very impressed.

The train on which the Liverpool quartet filmed *A Hard Day's Night* also regularly came through Bath, but we were always more interested in getting the number of the loco heading it rather than espying the train's illustrious working passengers. About ten years ago I went to the Theatre Royal to a Sunday night *Sounds of the Sixties* performance with various artists. The ageing Searchers were on last and began their set by saying that the last time they had been in Bath was at the Pavilion all those years ago. "I was there," proudly exclaimed a leather-jacketed, pony-tailed yet balding man with middle age spread a few seats to our left. "So was I," shouted someone similar from the stalls. "Me too," joined in a voice from the Upper Circle. Should I too proclaim to the gathered audience my presence at this distant event in this rather ostentatious way? A sideways glance at my teenage children, who were the youngest there by about thirty years and who were showing somewhat bemused embarrassment at the antics of their elders, persuaded me against such a public display of fellowship, and anyway the band launched into *Needles and Pins* and spared me any more soul searching. So I would like the said *Needles and Pins* as disc number five to record my very peripheral experience of the swinging Sixties.

Straightaway my sixth choice please, to register my real musical taste of the time – rock and roll, and a Chuck Berry song *Promised Land*, sung by Elvis Presley, would encapsulate it all. A while before the British groups of the Sixties exploded onto the scene we had been totally seduced by the sheer and novel thrill of American music from Fats Domino, Gene Vincent, Jerry Lee Lewis, Little Richard, Del Shannon, Don and Phil Everly and, of course, the King, Elvis. I never mastered the Jive, I didn't rip up cinema seats or sport a knuckleduster and the closest I came to being a teddy boy was an indulgence in a short lived fad for luminous green or orange socks but it was rock and roll and the sounds of the late Fifties which set our musical agenda and our toes a-tapping.

My arrival at King Edward's School about this time led indirectly to my being given the name Blocker which has stuck with me ever since. At Hampset I have always been known by this title and everyone assumes that it must be a reference to my, for want of a better word, batting. This, however, is as big a misconception as the one which assumes that the Hampset logo of a Scorpion is a reference to a sting in the tail, homage paid to the exploits of generations of lower order batsmen. It might have become this but this is certainly not what the founders and originators intended. The truth is much more scabrous. Ken Saunders and Brian Martin, having hit upon the hybrid name of Hampset, as an amalgam of their respective counties, were idly thumbing through a book on astrology in the CBBS library one day in the gloomy days of war-torn 1940 and found that parts of the body were supposedly influenced by signs of the zodiac.

Our mentor and co-founder of the club Ken Saunders resplendently sporting a club blazer with the scorpion motif but, on this occasion, no cravat.

I leave it to your imagination to work out which corporal entity was influenced by the scorpion and the information was so appealing that the dangerous insect was adopted as the nascent club's insignia and has been proudly sported ever since by members, most of whom have surely been unaware of the origins of the badge they wear.

A similarly misconstrued provenance is attached to the name Blocker. On the staff of King Edward's at the time was a master who delighted in giving each of his pupils a nickname which he thought was appropriate to the individual, some of which have no doubt stayed with their owners for life. 'Duster' Dowson was a geography teacher and his own sobriquet had been bestowed on him to some extent, no doubt, for reasons of euphony but mostly because of a complete inability in him ever to locate a board rubber in any of the rooms in which he taught. This might have been because they were constantly hidden by the inhabitants of the rooms, but why he never simply carried one around with him I shall never know. As a geography teacher he spent most of his time drawing on the blackboard complicated coloured diagrams in a range of chalks wider than any artist's palette. To erase these completely or perhaps make alterations to them Duster would simply use his voluminous gown of the sort in which all masters taught in those days. Wherever he went within the school and perhaps even outside for all we knew he was accompanied by a cloud of fine, multi-coloured chalk dust which over the years cannot have done much good to his lungs or those of all with whom he came into contact.

He must have been quite a good geography teacher for I can still recall the capital cities of most countries, or at least those which existed before about 1960, for that was the old-fashioned type of geography we learnt at the time, and I can even more vividly recall the fascinating features such as basket of eggs topography, ox-bow lakes, terminal moraine and roches moutonnées, as depicted in Duster's fascinating diagrams. Soon after arriving in school my brother had been sucking his fountain pen too assiduously in a geography lesson, so great was the concentration on a cross section of a river delta or a glacial valley chalked up before him, that he ended up with his mouth covered in dark blue Quink. From then on he was known as 'Inky' Johnson and when a younger, shorter and rather more rotund version appeared on the First Form wooden benches he was immediately christened 'Blot'. This original and correct version followed me through my school career but almost as soon as it became known amongst my Hampset friends it was corrupted, either by chance or design, into 'Blocker', a fitting encapsulation of my limited batting prowess which must have already been apparent to the discerning eye. And 'Blocker' it has remained.

'Duster', when we got to about the Under-14s, also took us for rugby. He was a great believer in fitness and all those either in or on the fringes of the school team at this level, I suppose it would be termed 'in the squad' nowadays, were required on games afternoons (Tuesdays and Thursdays) to run from Broad Street, where we were still housed, along Pulteney Street, up to the canal and then all along its bank to the playing fields in Bathampton, whilst all the weeds and bookworms were transported to their fields of boredom in a spluttering double-decker bus. And that was not the end of it. After a practice session we were then told to run all the way back. Duster would give us a bit of a start and then set off in pursuit, perhaps to keep himself in shape for his marathon chalk-drawing sessions, but anyone he overtook had to repeat the whole exercise the following day after school. Nowadays it seems like an exercise in complete sadism but it taught you camouflage skills in that the trick was to hide somewhere along the canal bank until the dreaded 'Duster' powered past and then saunter at leisure back to Broad Street, making sure that you entered unnoticed via the back gate. It was also a massive incentive not to get into any team or anywhere near it. In my case, a free Saturday afternoon could always be better spent with some of my Hampset friends watching Bristol Rovers. It also gave me a life-long antipathy for rugby.

On one glorious afternoon 'Duster' was himself unable to complete the return run. During the course of the practice period he became more and more exasperated by our funking inability to tackle. We had in the school at the time an excellent rugby player in Geoff Frankcom, a contemporary of my brother, who, in a year or two from this, gained a Cambridge blue and a couple of England caps playing in the centre. Faced with our pathetic attempts to stop our opponents at speed, 'Duster' summoned the fledgling international from an adjacent pitch and ordered him to demonstrate how to tackle. Our coach explained that he would run several times at this budding English centre who would show us how to tackle from a variety of angles. He grabbed the ball and pounded towards the try line only to be felled so ferociously by the demonstrator that he ended up prostrate on the pitch, unable to continue the session and certainly in no fit state to chase us back along the canal bank. Our chastened rugby coach had to stagger onto the school bus and journey back to Broad Street in less athletic a fashion than normal whilst we could amble our way towards the same destination still chortling at the demise of our mentor. A question of *Kes* at K.E.S., I feel.

A few years earlier the King Edward's playing fields at Bathampton had also been the scene of a short spell of acute unease for my father, but not of physical discomfort. At the end of my brother's first year at the school we were invited, with all the other families, to Sports Day which was held on the last Saturday of the summer term. It turned out to be a gloriously sunny July day. My father somehow wangled the afternoon off from his grocery duties and off we set, mostly to watch my brother perform for his House in the 'throwing the cricket ball' event, my father in his demob suit, a broad-striped, chocolate brown affair, my mother in her best (and only) summer dress and me looking as respectable as possible. In all the careful preparation of our appearance my father had forgotten his wallet, a fact which was only discovered when we were already half way to the Bear Flat on the bus. Between them my parents managed to muster enough coins for the return bus fare but we were left completely bereft of funds. On arrival at the Sports we were ushered into a very large, imposing marquee and there we were offered tea in china cups stamped with a crest and something we took to be Latin, salmon and cucumber sandwiches, fancy cakes and chocolate biscuits made more exclusive by being wrapped in silver paper. My father was convinced we would have to pay and pay highly for such fare, for in his book no-one ever gave you anything for nothing. How would we pay when someone came around demanding settlement of our account? "Don't have anything," he whispered desperately out of the side of his mouth but plates were proffered, trays of food were brought out and it was impossible sullenly to refuse and not to partake at all. We tried to concentrate on the athletic events but more and more succulent goodies came round. My father's discomfort grew, how could we extricate ourselves from this? We could perhaps in turn creep out to the 'lav', wherever that was, and, having regrouped, hot-foot it across open ground to the sanctuary of some trees which lined the canal bank or perhaps we could flatten ourselves and crawl, infantryman-like, under the sides of the tent and away. We might feign illness and all be transported to safety in an ambulance. None of these hastily conceived, panic-stricken plans proved practical and we were left to squirm, as we were plied with food and drink, awaiting the time of financial reckoning. My father kept peering around, trying to pick out the person who must have been put in charge of settling accounts, for maybe we could manage to avoid him by deploying some of the same tactics as those used to dodge the man who collected the deckchair dues at Weymouth or Weston. But no-one came, the Sports seemed to be coming to an end, people started to drift away to their vehicles, my brother joined us briefly before heading off with the other boys to get the school bus back to Broad Street where they had to register before being dismissed and we had to pretend that we had watched him come third in the First Form cricket ball hurling event. Still no-one demanded money and we walked, as casually and nonchalantly as possible, towards the bus stop by the canal bridge.

Our embarrassment was not over yet though. Everyone else had evaporated in cars and we were left waiting for one of the infrequent no. 14s which linked Bathampton to the city centre when a large car nosed its way out through the white wooden gate and stopped. A figure descended to shut the gate behind them. It was one W.E. Willetts, the Deputy Head, and in the passenger seat sat the imposing figure of Mr H.M. Porter, the Head Master, who was reputed to feel great animosity towards the motor car but who, on this occasion, had presumably swallowed his principles and had accepted a ride in his second-in-command's staff car. "Would you like a lift into town?" enquired Willetts. More discomfort, but we could hardly refuse and in we clambered, sinking into the plush leather seats. At least I didn't have to respond to any of the attempts at conversation by the two grandees in the front. It was left to my parents to remember to pronounce their aitches and to use long words. For them the relatively short journey into Bath must have seemed endless. "They were very nice though," opined my mother when she related the whole afternoon later to Aunty Floss, as if she naturally assumed that all of her social superiors would not be 'nice'. Since that beautiful July day in the early fifties I must have been to countless school Sports Days. I've never liked them.

My own schooldays at King Edward's were perfectly happy ones. I learnt a lot, made good progress, as a scholarship boy should, and eventually left for a good university. There was certainly no mistreatment or bullying, but I never really quite felt at home. I rarely accepted invitations to other boys' much grander houses, since I would have felt embarrassed to reciprocate and entertain them in our prefab. All in all I just felt more at home amongst my own kind and increasingly this meant 'over Hampset'.

King Edward's School, Bath First Eleven in about 1960.

The only side in which my brother and I featured together.

My brother, as captain, is in the middle of the front row, flanked on his left by Jack Deverell, who went on to an illustrious career in the Army, and on his right by Bob Hayter, who became a good local cricketer for Bath and Bath Civil Service.

The somewhat rotund younger Johnson is on the far right of the back row. The captain probably did not often put this junior figure onto bowl, more likely he was made to do all the fielding, as in the early days at 'the Players'. Racing round the outfield, however, might have done his shape some good.

A cricketing apprenticeship

By the time I got to secondary school I was already well established in the junior ranks of Hampset Cricket Club. I graduated fairly quickly from the outfield exercises to the more intensely practical instruction given out in the nets and there came under the guidance of Ken Saunders, one of the co-founders of the club. A severe back disability had already seriously compromised his own ability to play. He still turned out for the Seconds and managed to bowl a few overs with the jerky movements of an automaton.

He was always immaculately turned out. This included the sporting of a cravat, in club colours of course, the famous scorpion to the fore. He could stay in and bat with great resolution, but a lack of movement meant that he scored at an extremely snail-like rate, valuable if the innings got into trouble but frustrating for those who had to risk all to try to keep the scoreboard ticking over. Plots were hatched at times to run Ken out deliberately, but nobody quite dared carry through such an audacious undertaking. I am sure that Ken realised he could no longer influence things on the pitch himself, and he saw in us youngsters a way of continuing his legacy, of ensuring that what he had helped to create developed and prospered. Under 'Gruffo's' tuition we learnt the valuable basics, the virtues of line and length when bowling, of playing with an immaculate straight bat when at the crease and of doing things efficiently but unspectacularly when in the field. Nothing was designed to annoy him more than to see someone attempting to take a catch one-handed or, even worse, using their boot to stop the ball. He also fulminated against all the noise on the field which was creeping in even at our level, railing, for example, against lavish praise being heaped on a fielder who managed to cut off a ball "which my grandmother could have stopped – and she's dead!"

Getting in line when batting was also deemed an absolute essential, and to this end he erected on the leg side of the nets a contraption involving the sharp end of a stump designed to give a sharp prod to any fledgling batsman who was tempted to back away to leg. Such a Heath Robinson device would surely fall foul of Health and Safety and even Child Protection regulations nowadays but it worked – on everyone except me.

For bowlers he would chalk on the rubberoid surface what seemed like a miniscule rectangle on what he considered a correct length and demand that at least five balls out of six fall within this tiny space. He got me as a left-arm spinner to run up in a measured way in an arc around him at the bowler's end, rather than charge up straight in any demented fashion.

Ken was a great coach, but at times he slightly lost sight of reality with the objects of his instruction. He took upon himself to instil in me all the subtleties and mysteries of being a 'slow left-armer', and to this end he opined that anyone taking on this role should bowl 47 identical stock balls of impeccable line and length and then surprise the batsman with some unspecified variation. "You've done a great job for your captain," he would say "if you return figures of 25 overs, 4 for 75." The underlying truth of this was no doubt sound for a test bowler but it was not much good for a schoolboy cricketer who was lucky to get two or three overs in a game. Nevertheless, I decided to adapt this to more practical circumstances and resolved to adopt a pattern for every over. I would bowl four of 'Gruffo's' stock balls to begin with, then the fifth would still be the conventional left-arm finger spinner's leg-break but either delivered wide of the crease and directed into the batsman's pads or sent down from 23 yards, and the sixth and last ball would be an 'arm ball', if I could perfect such a weapon. I continued to bowl exactly to this template for the next fifty years – but with one amendment which came slightly later.

The author receiving coaching from Ken Saunders in the nets. The splayed state of the stumps suggests that much remedial treatment is needed.

Early on in my First Eleven career we were journeying to play Bridgwater during a test series against India, listening to the ball-by-ball commentary on the radio as we went. The lunch interval came as we were passing through the village of Bawdrip and the Indian bowler Bishen Bedi, he of the wonderfully coloured turbans, was interviewed. He revealed that a ball which got him many wickets was one which he delivered with his fingers wrapped a bit more over the top of the seam than usual. The Indian wizard claimed that this produced a delivery which had top spin on it but which, more dangerously from the batsman's point of view, dipped in flight quite late in its trajectory. I decided to try it and, after a while working on it, I found that it worked in the way that had been outlined. Thus was born the Bishen Bedi Bawdrip Ball, which became delivery no. 4 in each over's repertoire.

From then on the pattern never changed, irrespective of who was in or the pitch and the weather conditions. For the rest of my career I produced in every over, and there were roughly ten thousand of them, three stock balls, the Bishen Bedi ball, one delivered wide of the crease and the 'arm ball' to finish. Occasionally a captain or another colleague or team-mate would question the wisdom of this rigid sequence. Most vociferous in his comments was Stan Szczotko. "Look, Blocker," he would reason, "every batsman in the South-West of England knows what you do by now." "Ah, but Stan, that's the point," I rejoined. "It's double bluff, Stan. 'Surely,' they say to themselves, 'he can't be so daft as to keep doing the same old thing,' and they are constantly looking for something different." I'm not sure Stan was convinced, but I carried on anyway; at least the series of excellent wicketkeepers I played with over the years knew what was happening. Very, very occasionally, if a batsman had been in for a long time, I would send down an 'arm ball' first ball, but it usually strayed down the leg side and was dispatched over the mid-wicket boundary. I was more likely to be unnerved by my own flirting with innovation than the batsman it was supposed to bamboozle. Invariably I reverted to my tried and tested system.

Inevitably Ken Saunders played a less prominent role in club affairs as he grew older. He never recovered, I feel, from the loss of his wife at a relatively early age, and he himself died when still by no means old. Nobody, however, had such an influence on the generation of club cricketers which produced arguably the years of greatest success for Hampset. There was nothing particularly revolutionary or innovative in what he said; he merely drilled into us the old-fashioned virtues which even today would stand any young cricketer in very good stead.

I began going to the ground at times other than practice evenings. On match days I sat and watched those who coached us putting their recommendations into practice with varying degrees of success, learning along the way that people do not always in reality practise what they preach. Bill Barrett and I began to help with the scoring. In those days there was nothing at all mechanical and certainly nothing remotely electronic about the Hampset scoreboard. White numbers painted on black metal rectangles, taken from neatly arranged piles at the foot of the board, had simply to be hung onto hooks and nails. In performing this task we were helpers to the official scorer, the original secretary of the club, Michael Stevens. To my knowledge he had not played much himself, but he was an excellent scorer and statistician.

On match days we would meet up with Michael at the pavilion and then proceed to the top of the ground in his wake. Ahead of us he made his way purposefully towards his centre of operations, carrying a fairly substantial canvas hold-all, the contents of which clinked as he walked. At first I naively thought that this noise must be caused by bottles of Quink of different colours, essential materials for the art of scoring. But then I realised that he only ever used black ink and discovered that the clinking came from a glass and a considerable number of bottles of Guinness, which were needed to sustain him through the afternoon's record keeping. However many glasses of the dark liquid topped by a creamy froth he consumed, the standard of the entries in his scorebook, completed in wonderfully neat, copper-plate handwriting, never wavered.

Michael, or 'Nag' as he was known, eventually succumbed to the demon drink and was succeeded by a series of scorers, the most notable of whom during my playing days was Frank Mines who also had a penchant for a good pint of beer but not whilst on duty in the scorebox. Frank reserved his imbibing for the pavilion after the game when his book and match report were complete. It was Frank who began the habit of using a galaxy of coloured pens. From his neat variegated score sheets at the end of the day one could glean all sorts of information on what had happened during any innings, simply by interpreting the colour code – if you were in the know, that is. Frank rarely made the slightest error and he was virtually unflappable. About the only time I saw him panic was when he was on his own in the scorebox for a match against Frome, the opposition having arrived without a scorer, a most unusual occurrence for them. Unfortunately there were about six or seven Dredges in the side that day, and even then a couple of the said family had apparently been unavailable. Frank's cry from the box of "Bowler's name please?" or "Catcher's name please?" constantly yielded the same response: "Dredge." In the end we suggested he put down 'Dredge' for everything, leaving a gap for a suitable initial to be inserted later in the clubhouse.

One day when I turned up on my own to help the Guinness-supping scorer at a First Team match, Bill Barrett having already made it to the Second Eleven, I was met by a harassed looking captain, John Bell, who was by now our main coach. "Can you get your kit? We might be one short." Off I sped on my bike to gather up what kit I could find. By the time I returned I was sure the missing player would have turned up and I would not be required. But no, Andrew Pollock, a young Woodbine-smoking Maths teacher who had recently taken up a post in a Swindon school and who normally played for the second string, had broken irreparably down somewhere on the A4 and definitely would not make it. Faute de mieux I was about to take part in my first ever adult match for Hampset and in the senior side too. I have only hazy recollections of the game itself. I am pretty sure we lost. I went to the wicket but fortunately did not have to receive a ball; Jack Simmons, my predecessor as a genuine no. 11, was out before I had to face that particular trial. I ran around the field, mostly retrieving balls which had gone beyond the boundary, and 'Dinger' gave me an over at the end when the game was as good as lost. Not a glorious start, but a start nevertheless.

I had to wait sometime before my next appearance, in the Second Eleven, of course, but one day the summoning postcard arrived. Today, I imagine, most players learn of their selection by e-mail or text message or some other instantaneous method of communication, but then one received via Royal Mail a pre-printed postcard with gaps on it for the relevant details to be inserted. This was by no means as peremptory as the handwritten note scrawled by W.G. Grace which Brian Petty unearthed in a boot sale: 'You have been selected for Gloucestershire on Wednesday. Be there,' it ran. The Hampset version went something as follows: 'You have been selected for the ...... XI to play against ...... on Saturday/Sunday (delete as appropriate) at Bloomfield Rise/Away. Meet at ...... am/pm at the ground/the Bear Flat.' I never understood why, for years, we continued the tradition of meeting for away games at the Bear Flat. Of course it was a habit born in the early years when the Club had been formed by pupils at the CBBS situated on nearby Beechen Cliff at a time when all games were played away, the Bloomfield Rise site as yet not having been acquired. By the time I started playing, however, we all mostly lived on Odd Down and we had to catch a bus to the Bear Flat, only to transfer to a series of cars in which we almost certainly retraced our steps back up the hill, since virtually all our away matches took place to the South and West of the city. It was only after many years that the meeting-place was more sensibly changed to the ground at Bloomfield Rise.

The beginning of my playing career coincided with the end of travelling to away fixtures by coach. I managed just one of these outings. On this occasion the Sunday destination was Yeovil, to the appropriately named Johnson Park. The Fales Coaches of Combe Down charabanc duly arrived at the appointed time – on the Bear Flat, of course. On we all piled, players, wives, girlfriends and supporters for a real excursion with the game and then fish and chips, a pub stop and much out-of-tune singing on the way back. It was not long before club members acquired cars, and the coach was no longer needed. More convenient, I suppose, but less fun.

At about the time I made my fortuitous debut Alan Telford and John Bell emerge from the old pavilion to open the innings, at quite a late stage, to judge from the clock. The white picket fence has not yet been replaced by the low Bath stone wall which is still standing today. This wall was constructed by no less a mason than Cyril Beazer, founder and owner of the famous Bath building firm, aided, or perhaps hindered, by a youthful group of keen but incompetent helpers.

When I was about 14 years old one of the 'You have been selected' postcards popped through the prefab letter box: Second Eleven, Away to Stratton-on-the-Fosse on the following Sunday. We played on one of the back pitches of Downside School in the aforesaid Somerset village. The only thing I can remember of the encounter was an unfortunate incident of an ecclesiastical nature. We were in the field after tea. The older members of the team who had played before in this imposing setting in the shadow of Downside Abbey were well aware of the tradition which accompanied the tolling of the angelus bell at 6 pm, when play was halted and players reverentially turned towards the Abbey, but no-one had bothered to tell us younger members of the side. At the appointed time the bell solemnly began to ring out across the peaceful countryside, and play was suspended. Bill Barrett, however, continued to patrol the covers, proudly sporting his recently acquired Hampset cap. At the time we had a rather rough-and-ready captain called Ernie Shellard, and the respectful silence was suddenly shattered by a stentorian voice calling out "Oy, you boy, take thee f………. 'at off." Any monks in earshot were presumably not amused.

Decades later I returned several times to Downside with school sides from Dauntsey's as schoolmaster and umpire. On the last occasion, shortly before I retired from teaching, having sunk from being in charge of the school's First Eleven to a much lowlier rank, I was officiating in an epic encounter between the Dauntsey's Fourth Eleven and Downside's Under-16 Bs. At this level it is often nearly impossible to find eleven people to put into the field, leave alone a scorer willing to give up their Saturday afternoon, unless you can persuade a girl who at the time is enamoured of one of the players to come along. Even then there is a good chance she will be 'challenged' in literacy and numeracy and will almost certainly be more intent on exhibiting her charms to her latest beau than on keeping an accurate record of proceedings she does not understand. All in all it is usually better to do it yourself.

So, on this occasion, as happened quite often, I was keeping score whilst umpiring at the same time. Downside had obviously had similar manpower problems and had press-ganged one of their Spanish boarders into service in a playing capacity. We had reduced Downside to about 60 for nine, Extras 38, a typical total in these circumstances, and the unfortunate Spaniard approached the wicket. None of his borrowed kit fitted and he was wearing only one pad. He was brandishing a bat with one hand and with the other was clutching his groin; someone had evidently told him he needed to wear something to protect his manhood but had failed to explain that this weird box-like contraption needed to be slipped inside a jock strap. He was thus fighting a losing battle to stop the abdominal protector from sinking down his trouser leg. He looked as sorry a sight as a rookie bullfighter thrust into an arena with a snorting bull for company. Warily he came to my end, since the previous batsman had been dismissed by the last ball of an over. "Name, please," I enquired, in an attempt to keep an accurate record of the proceedings for posterity. "Qué?" came the reply, reminiscent of Manuel in *Fawlty Towers*. "What is your name?" I asked, taking care to articulate as clearly as possible. I just caught "Ignacio" and the rest of his name went on for about 30 seconds. Presumably the son of some grandee with a lengthy title. 'Spanish boy,' I inserted against 'Batsman no. 11'.

The ball was delivered, yet another wide, which eluded the wicketkeeper and first slip and rolled gently towards third man. Although it was strictly not his call – no niceties here – the striker took control of the situation and shouted "Run!" "Where I run?" shrieked Ignacio to all and sundry and, perhaps having once seen a game of baseball or rounders, set off at right angles to me, still trying to rein in his errant box. In the ensuing chaos even the Fourth Eleven managed to run him out. 60 all out – something to bowl at, at least at this level. We got to 50-odd for nine and the angelus rang out. First ball after resumption our no. 11 was bowled for a golden duck by the only delivery directed at the stumps all afternoon. "That bell, it broke my concentration, sir," explained the disconsolate batsman by way of apology, as we trudged back towards the pavilion. Rather rudely I made no reply. I was miles away, recalling another incident involving the same bell some forty years before.

Regular appearances in the seconds followed over the next couple of years, for the club was not exactly flush with players. In the early sixties the team was an odd amalgam of the young and the old, as, I suppose, is the case with many second string and lesser sides in any club. Representing raw youth were Bill Barrett, John Nicholas, Sam Shearn, John Stevens, Dick Stickells, myself and a few others.

Several people had a go at captaining this rag, tag and bobtail outfit. Bernard King was probably the most notable of these, for he did everything at breakneck speed. He would, for example, run in to bat, often without any gloves, take one sighter and then attempt to hit every ball, irrespective of its merits, out of the ground. If he really got his eye in and stayed at the crease for any length of time, the total shot up, but this happened only once in a blue moon. He did connect more often than not, but virtually every delivery was sent spiralling skywards and second eleven fielders dropped the majority of these as they plummeted earthwards, often, it seemed, with ice on them. After a while, though, one stuck and the skipper had produced yet another cameo, 20 or 30 in about a dozen balls at most. In the field Bernard kept everyone on their toes by a combination of eccentric field placings and unfathomable bowling changes. He gave the impression that he knew exactly what he was doing and that the rest of us were simply not following the plot. I suspect now that this was not the case. Bernard's driving was a bit like his batting, fast and furious. All other road users were viewed as a nuisance, and attempts at overtaking were always accompanied by a strange rocking backwards and forwards motion and by derogatory comments about his adversary, as he willed his car to get past that of the other motorist who refused to give way.

We travelled around in a variety of vehicles. George Dunn, a burly fellow with large hands, was one of the opening bowlers, although he could rarely be deployed immediately, as he always arrived late. He was a rep for some sort of agricultural suppliers and the back seat of his spacious car, which young cricketers were often asked to share, was usually full of samples of pig feed or sheep dip. After a while he must have decided that he would be better at putting his products to use than at selling them and he took himself off to Ireland to farm some corner of the Emerald Isle, thus depriving us of his bustling, quickish bowling. George's fellow opening bowler, Cyril Butler, had a rather natty, two-tone, red and white coupé, which just about had enough room behind the two front seats for a small cricketer laid out prone with a pile of kit, not the most comfortable way to journey to a game. Cyril was somewhat rotund and worked for the railways in some capacity, organising freight and parcels, and he came puffing up to the wicket in much the same way as one of the engines which delivered the goods he oversaw, his right arm pumping like a piston rod. He was capable, however, of regularly producing the most exaggeratedly swinging deliveries I have ever seen which quite often defeated the batsman and the wicketkeeper before ending up over the third man or the fine leg boundary. Cyril's batting was eccentrically ineffectual and I had some work to do to supplant him as the resident no. 11.

What F.E.L. Titchener's initials meant remained a mystery, for no-one ever got to know his real name. He was universally and for ever known as 'Titch' and he was able, when selected, to transport most of the side, because he had a large vehicle of the type known at the time, I believe, as a 'shooting-brake'. Possession of this lumbering wagon might sometimes have been the reason for his inclusion. Unfortunately for fellow travellers Titch was something to do with the motor trade, and passengers regularly had to share the generous amount of room in the back of his car with old tyres, petrol cans, disused number plates and other automobile accessories. Titch's reputation went before him, and we were dying to make his acquaintance long before we actually met him and became one of his team-mates, for Titch had been a Battle of Britain pilot, one of 'The Few', who had apparently received several commendations and decorations for shooting down enemy aces. We, who had been brought up on comic book stereotypes, were expecting a dapper, smartly-dressed, upright fellow with a striking moustache, who spoke with a clipped, upper-crust accent, a suave action man with a string of kills of Messerschmitts and Fokkers to his name, smoking Dunhill cigarettes in a long cigarette holder. The reality was entirely the opposite for Titch was a shy, diffident person with a fairly severe stutter. He was invariably dressed in an old sports jacket with leather patches on the elbows and crumpled trousers. He drove his 'shooting-brake' around at a very pedestrian pace, as if he was scared of it. How, we wondered, had Titch helped to repel the might of Herr Goering's Luftwaffe?

If Titch was sedate, a fellow early order batsman, Bill Seabrook, was the exact opposite, for he leapt around the crease like a demented rabbit. He defied all received wisdom about batting technique, but amazingly more often than not made effective contact with the ball, much to the consternation of opposing bowlers. If Titch and Bill were batting together the combination of frenetic frolics and stammering diffidence led almost always to an inexorable conclusion – a run-out. Never have so many run-outs been caused so often in so few matches, as Mr Churchill might have put it.

One of the Second Eleven stalwarts of the time who could not transport us around, for I am certain he did not drive, was the irascible, ruddy complexioned dentist George Davis, who had been with the Club from the earliest days. As I got to know him better I came to think that his ill-tempered crabbedness was an affectation and that deep down he was good-hearted; certainly his long-suffering wife was. Perhaps his outward gruffness stemmed from having spent his life peering into people's mouths, dealing with diseased teeth which were all too common then. George did not seem to treat children and youngsters with the slightest degree of patience and understanding, which was something of a drawback since he was the Bath schools' dentist and we were wary of upsetting him. The hapless Kenny Bodman had, during the week prior to one of his first Hampset appearances, undergone an inspection of his teeth by George at

George Davis – the quick-tempered puller and driller of childish teeth.

school and in the game had the misfortune to run the rubicund dentist out before he had scored. Fulminating back in the pavilion George was heard to state in no uncertain terms that the next time he got the little bastard in the chair he would pull all his teeth out. We believed him.

A bit later on in its history the Second Eleven possessed a secret weapon, a trump card but one which they could play only once with each opposition, in the shape of Fred Narain, whose playing career came slightly later than those mentioned above and was fairly short-lived.

Fred came from Guyana, I believe, and, like many West Indians from the colonies and ex-colonies, had come to this country to join our forces during the war. In Fred's case I think it was the RAF, and he had not returned to his native land at the end of hostilities. Fred had married a local lady and had come to live at the bottom of the ground in the short offshoot from Bloomfield Drive which, rather curiously, forms part of Bloomfield Rise and had naturally become a member of the club which was so close to his home. Fred must have been one of the first black residents of Odd Down.

Fred's short playing career coincided with the time when West Indian cricket was in the ascendancy and everyone from the Caribbean was assumed to be as lithe, athletic and incredibly gifted when wielding a rapier-like bat or when sending down lightning fast, unplayable deliveries as the first-class cricketers whose exploits thrilled and impressed us. Fred, however, was the very antithesis of this. He was what for a West Indian cricketer seemed almost a contradiction in terms: uncoordinated, clumsy and inept. The thought of Fred powering through a 100-yard sprint or engaging in limbo dancing was frankly laughable. But opposition members who had never encountered Fred were not to know this.

Our secret weapon was drafted in if we were short and, when we turned up at away venues or when they arrived at Bloomfield Rise and saw Fred immaculately turned out in cream flannels and shirt and with beautifully whitened boots, they immediately assumed they were in for a drubbing with either bat or ball or both. We tried to get Fred to have a steel toecap fixed to one of his boots to increase the opposition's discomfort by giving them the impression that they were about to face a demon paceman but he never took up the suggestion. If Hampset batted first and Fred was either not required or came in late, probably only to face a few balls before getting out, our opponents' apprehension was only increased. He could only be a fierce bowler about to unleash his venom on their unfortunate upper order and this must surely have spoilt many an appetite during the tea interval. If, on the other hand, Hampset fielded first and Fred was seen to spill a few easy chances or, if he was given a token bowl towards the end of the innings and had delivered a series of high, looping and totally innocuous balls which did nothing through the air or off the pitch, the obvious conclusion was that he was a dashing, hard-hitting batsman who was about to put their bowlers to the sword. None of these forebodings ever came to pass but for sowing doubt and trepidation in opponents' minds Fred was worth his weight in gold.

After a few seasons it came to be generally realised that Fred was no lithe, athletic cricketing wonder and, having lost some of his potency as a shock-trooper, he decided to hang up his nearly pristine boots and he devoted himself to serving the club in other capacities. In one of these roles he became the organiser of teas. In the pursuance of these duties Fred must have been offered at some time an immense job lot of angel cake at a knock-down price and at home he must have had several freezers full of this delicacy, for it appeared on our tea tables in copious quantities for what seemed like years and years. Ever since I have never quite been able to view the offer of angel cake with any more enthusiasm than that of dried egg powder or Camp coffee. In all other ways Fred's teas were delicious and, come high summer, when a certain temperature was reached, he would deem it time to bring forth his tour de force: exotic fruit salad and ice cream.

Rather strangely for a West Indian, Fred was no great lover of excessively hot days and this seemed to be a genetic inheritance for in one of those long, hot summers of the mid-seventies his father came over to visit him and constantly complained about the weather. Narain senior was even blacker than Fred but he spent most of his time in the UK ensconced in the shade of a big tree at the bottom of the ground, his head protected by a giant straw hat. Perhaps Odd Down, at such times, did not have the same sort of heat to which he was used. Hampset's other great West Indian, Eric Worrell, seemed to share this antipathy towards hot weather. On one blisteringly hot day at Chard, for example, Eric announced that the heat was in fact too great for him to bat early on and he had to seek comfort in the cool of the dressing room until the sun had sunk a little more towards the West. He went in about number seven and insisted on scoring his runs, and there were quite a few of them, only in boundaries.

It was in the company of a diverse set of people that, for a few years in the Second Eleven, we learnt our trade, blossoming as club cricketers and, more importantly, learning a lot about people and life along the way.

Our apprenticeship, however was not confined to the cricket pitch. In season, out of season, in the evenings, during school holidays, I began to spend more and more time over ''ampset'. At least my parents knew where I was all the time. We quickly learnt that, as members of a club with limited resources and whose aim, right from the beginning, had been to provide a good standard of cricket at affordable rates, if we wanted good facilities and conditions in which to play, we had to help provide them ourselves. And so we started to muck in, keeping the surrounds well maintained, helping Rosey prepare the wickets. In an era when we had no motor roller, we joined bands of volunteers who pushed and pulled a series of different sized manual rollers to and fro for hours across the square, swapping cricketing stories and experiences as we went. Above all, we mowed the outfield.

The latter activity was accomplished with an ancient, temperamental motor mower, of a sort on which 'Burfy' would probably not have been seen dead. This contraption was started by means of a large brass starting-handle. It rarely coughed its way into life first time and it sometimes took an inordinate number of exhausting swings of the handle to get it reluctantly to splutter into operation. When in a particularly morose mood, it could give its subservient attendant a vicious, wrist endangering kick-back. Once going, however, and at work in the outfield, it proved a very capable machine. It cooperated willingly with our experiments at cutting alternately light and dark circles or stripes, as we saw on first-class and test match grounds and readily sped us to the northern side of the ground where we dumped the grass clippings in a large heap, which developed over time into a slimy, malodorous, steaming expanse, as Cyril Butler, he of the pumping bowling arm action, found to his cost one day when he toppled into it when attempting to catch a steepling drive at long-on. He emerged bespattered and definitely not smelling of roses.

In the winter months we played and watched football, activities which we zealously pursued when most of us went off to rugby playing secondary schools. To show and practise a preference for the round ball often became in these surroundings an act of teenage rebellion. At first the venue for watching matches was Twerton Park, home to the black and white striped Bath City and where on a few occasions we witnessed giant-killing cup action but we soon branched out further afield to Eastville and Bristol Rovers.

August 2010 and Bill Barrett, now resident in Weston-super-Mare and still a regular Pirates follower, and I decide to relive old memories and attend an early season Rovers game together. I get a train from Westbury to Temple Meads in the company of a few Southampton supporters and the usual passenger list of young unaccompanied teenage mothers armed with a mobile phone and an ignored infant in a pushchair. I'm picked up from the station and we head north past the old Eastville ground, replaced now by a superstore and attendant car park, a monument to modernity set in a space where once greyhounds raced, footballers plied their trade and one young set of Bathonians came to be excited by their efforts. A bit further on towards the schizophrenic Memorial Stadium, home at one and the same time to two seemingly incompatible footballing codes, we turn off into a short road leading to a well-known DIY superstore where the street-wise Barrett claims you can usually find a parking space easily. We duly do so, right next to the nameplate of the road – Petherbridge Way. What a great omen! Am I to find, as we journey up the Muller Road, a network of offshoots to the main thoroughfare all bearing the names of our heroes of a bygone age? Will there be a Geoff Bradford Road, a direct, no-nonsense artery going straight to its destination or a decorative, inventive Alfie Biggs Avenue? Perhaps we'll find a short, explosive Peter Hooper Mews, a Bobby Jones Way and a Ray Mabbutt Crescent. Disappointingly, however, the walk up the hill to the stadium reveals no such side streets, not even a sinuous cul de sac, the Harold Jarman Alley.

Harold was an enigma, a right-winger who in equal measure charmed and frustrated the Eastville crowd. At times he was capable of producing dazzling runs, gliding past and leaving in his wake a trail of opposing defenders before sending over a cross of pin-point accuracy for a fellow forward to head home but at others he would hit the corner flag from about four yards out of an open goal or tamely surrender the ball, allowing the other side to pour forth from defence and threaten the Rovers' goal.

He was also an excellent cricketer who played at county level. He once came to Hampset, much to our discomfiture. Because most of our fixtures were with teams to the south of Bath, we mainly came across first class cricketers associated with Somerset but occasionally we came into contact with Gloucestershire men who were turning out for various Bristol clubs. Before the advent of Sunday League cricket there was much more scope for this to happen and their county clubs did not seem to mind them risking life and limb in a club match, perhaps they saw it as a way of getting some cheap practice. The redoubtable George Emmett came to Bloomfield Rise before my playing days and I witnessed him make an elegant century from in front of the scorebox, we were certainly kept busy that day with our metal-plated numbers. A couple of times when facing Almondsbury, we came up against David Allen after his England playing days were over but he opened the batting, rather than mesmerise us with his off-breaks. And then for the aptly named Gloucestershire Club and Ground side came Harold Jarman. Here I was bowling against the footballer I had so often watched from the terraces. His batting on this occasion proved to be a bit like his unpredictable football for at first the flying ex-winger looked a trifle vulnerable, perhaps even giving a couple of half chances as he progressed towards fifty, and we thought we were doing quite well to contain him but pride comes before a fall in cricket more than any activity for suddenly Harold cut loose and plundered his second half century in about 20 balls.

Back to August 2010. We reach the Memorial Stadium, have a drink in the supporters' club bar, settle on the halfway line behind the dugouts in the late summer sunshine, anticipating a satisfactory outcome. But things do not start well. Southampton score early on. The tactics seem a little naïve, Rovers with a couple of nimble forwards a bit short in stature pump long balls up into the Saints' penalty area for a couple of gargantuan centre backs to pick off at will. Three more times the visitors break away to score. Rovers lose 4-0 at home. The following Monday Southampton sack their manager, such are the vagaries of modern football.

The whole experience was a little different fifty years earlier, though the journey was again by train. It was not until considerably later that, particularly for evening games, we took to going to matches in John Bell's Morris Minor Traveller, which probably enjoyed the change, taking time off from delivering groceries. We would normally assemble at Bath Spa station, Bill Barrett, John Nicholas, myself and possibly a couple of others, all under the watchful, patient eye of John's dad, a keen, long-serving Rovers' supporter.

A local stopping train, bound probably for South Wales would take us all the way to Stapleton Road from where it was only a short walk to the ground, with opportunities to pick up an essential programme on the way at something less than the price charged nowadays. Sometimes in its haste to get to the tunnel and onwards to its eventual destination in the Principality, the Eastville flier would not bother to go into Temple Meads but, a little while after leaving the soon to be Beeching axed St. Anne's Halt, it would dive off to the right like a recalcitrant pupil playing truant through a mass of sidings and assembled goods wagons to emerge to the north of the central station, take a breather to see if it wasn't being followed at Lawrence Hill, and then deposit us, clad in our blue and white quartered scarves along with a lot of other Rovers' fans, at Stapleton Road. We made our way through the narrow clickety-clacking turnstiles, which John's dad's burly frame had some difficulty negotiating, and onto the terraces, there to stand in a swaying mass, straining on tip-toe once the match started to glimpse what was happening on the pitch.

Out of tune and out of key we bawled out at the tops of our voices that most incongruous of football anthems: *Goodnight Irene*, which is apparently all about crap – the gambling sort, I hasten to add. A couple of years ago Rovers had a decent cup run and acquitted themselves well at Derby County. The following day in the *Sunday Times* Richard Rae wrote of the Rovers' supporters' attempts to back their favourites in song: "Seldom can Irene have received her nocturnal farewells with such fervour." He obviously wasn't at the cup-tie, it must have been in the early sixties, when we drew with high-flying Aston Villa, Gerry Hitchens, just before his Italian days in Milan, et al. Sometimes in big games the crush on the terraces became too great for small boys and they were passed over adult heads to the safety of the pitch side. Thank goodness I never had to suffer such an indignity.

Being still of a fairly tender age, we did not venture too far afield to watch our favourites. Away matches at Swindon were an exception, for the railway town was easily accessible by train, as one would expect. We even on occasions went there just to watch the home team with no Rovers involvement at all. All this was just prior to the golden Summerbee, Hunt, Smart and Rogers era and I can recall nothing significant other than an incident in which Bill Barrett, who had repaired to the Station Hotel for a pee before getting the return train home and got lost in the Lounge Bar, had bumped into John Arlott and spilled his drink, Arlott's that is. Probably not a good idea.

The furthest we ever reached was Plymouth to see the Rovers take on the Argyle. Perhaps the fact that we lost 5-0 dissuaded us from further away excursions. On the long train journey back we fed ourselves on the indignation that the opposing centre-forward, George Kirby, who had scored a hat-trick, had blatantly punched in one of his goals. Not quite Maradona, but a cheating bastard all the same. The efficacy of referees' eyesight has been a perennial subject for discussion, more so on the whole than that of cricketing umpires who at times need even greater powers of observation. I tend to read newspapers from the back for it is there that one usually finds the sport and among the football results it is always the account of the Rovers' match that I look for first. For all those switchback days with the Rovers the next record has to be *Goodnight Irene,* whatever the lyrics might mean.

Days in the sun

After a short apprenticeship in the 'seconds' it was heady promotion to the First Eleven and forty-odd years of senior service. It has become a bit of a family joke as we've driven around the country and spotted signposts to fascinating sounding places that I've almost inevitably been able to say, "Oh, I've played cricket there." This ability to impress and then mostly vaguely to amuse my car-captive audience is all the more remarkable since almost all of such visits have been in the ranks of Hampset CC.

For a start there are all the places in the South West. We must have appeared in just about every nook and cranny in Bristol. I must say that most of the grounds here are unremarkable, functional rather than inherently attractive. However, I always enjoyed going to Keynsham, where we often encountered the Trescothicks, père et fils, usually much to our cost and, strangely enough, I liked going to Knowle, the ground that is, not so much the district. Some places around Bristol had a bit more to recommend them: Portishead, where huge ships bringing imported cars would occasionally glide past deep extra cover, and Claverham, under the flight path, where our antics on the ground must have given those taking off for the Costa del Sol a last glimpse of England, their England. Then there was Long Ashton from where you could watch the excursion trains taking eager-eyed families to a beach holiday at Weston-super-Mare and beyond but which got rather spoilt when they built the towering pillars of a by-pass in much greater proximity than the railway. There was Clevedon where, on a fine day, it was relaxing to stroll, while waiting to bat, to the top of Dial Hill and gaze across at the Welsh coast and mountains though more often than not, with a chilly gale blowing, one did not feel like going. I remember playing there on a particularly inhospitable Sunday, the day after the explosion at Tchernobyl, when a wind straight from the Urals was no doubt depositing radioactive fallout on us as, clad in several layers of jumpers, we sought to keep warm in the outfield. Weston-super-Mare provided a seaside venue but I always found it rather large and impersonal, especially since we usually spent a lot of time chasing leather in the capacious, sandy outfield. On the whole I looked forward more to visits to the more homely Uphill Castle just over the road, although the pleasurable experience of playing here could be tempered, on a day when the wind was in a particular direction, by the nearness of the local sewage works or some such evil-smelling plant.

Overall, although a lot more travelling was involved, I preferred going south and our years in the Somerset League, which coincided with times when we were at our strongest from the performance point of view, stand out for me as a golden era. Minehead was an exception for almost invariably we struggled for hours to get there on a June or July Saturday, getting stuck in queues of cars destined for the dubious delights of Butlin's and then, when we eventually got there, the game was fought out on an indifferent school pitch. Bridgwater was fine if the British Cellophane factory was shut down for its annual holiday. If not, it exuded the most disgusting smell known to the western world which somewhat spoilt the pleasure of playing next to it. Promotion and relegation, for us or for others, meant that we journeyed to a whole series of places to the south and west of our home base: Long Sutton, Milverton, Staplegrove, Ilminster, Watchet, where we once had to suspend play whilst the town's carnival floats assembled (no-one having informed the cricket club that this was the intention beforehand), Wellington, Evercreech, Wells, Burnham and all stations west, it seemed.

Burnham moved at one stage from one ground to another but for a couple of years had to play on a small, preparatory school ground. It was here that Bob Clapp, a redoubtable Sunday League performer for Somerset, emerged from a neighbouring garden to send down his swift deliveries. Of course, the Somerset League was centred on Taunton and we were sent into the fray against all the major sides in the County Town, to such an extent that it seemed at times that we were going to Taunton on every other Saturday. But it was worth it, although at the time I didn't have a wife to placate.

Firstly, there was Taunton Vale itself who played on the County Ground until they, like Burnham, had to move to another ground. In the days of the County Ground, however, until they revamped the facilities with a major facelift, there was the thrill of changing under the same hole in the roof which you knew had dripped rain into Botham's, Richards' or Garner's bag, just as it was doing to yours. Inevitably club games were played on the edge of the square so that the boundary on one side was quite short but on the other was ridiculously long. The trick, when fielding, was to get out onto the ground early, pushing unceremoniously past the captain, if necessary, to bag third man and mid-on on the short side. If an excuse was needed, you could always come up with: " I'd better go this side skip, I've got a bad arm and they'll run five to me on that side." I always had the team's best interests at heart and, anyway, 'anything for a quiet life' is the favourite adage for all spin bowlers.

During the game the fact that there were only about ten people and a stray mongrel watching our efforts in the home of Somerset cricket meant that the sound of bat on ball echoed eerily around the ground. At least, when they batted it appeared to do so with monotonous regularity. In the first year at Taunton's new ground, which was pretty large and unenclosed, an extremely officious neutral umpire told the home captain, Dennis Breakwell, a county cricketer of some standing, that he could not see the boundary rope from the middle and ordered him to fix bits of toilet paper to it at regular intervals. Breakwell was still fuming when they took the field and, for once, didn't run through us; he must have been concentrating on ways to annoy the umpire who had deigned to impose on him such a mundane task.

All in all, I think I found the Taunton Deane ground the most pleasant in the Somerset capital. Ominously for batsmen the ducks on the nearby river Tone would from time to time take off and fly over cricketing heads, seeming to wish to impose their names on individuals' scores. On one notable occasion the curse of the flying ducks worked in our favour. One car, containing the opening attack, was delayed and the home side had elected to bat. There's a lesson here, never put both opening bowlers, or batsmen for that matter, in the same vehicle, in the same way that the heir to the throne, I believe, never travels with the present incumbent. John Bissex, who was normally our first change, was given the new ball and, perhaps in the excitement of this unexpected responsibility, badly pulled a hamstring second ball. He refused all offers by others to finish the over for him. Instead, to complete the one over he was going to get that day, he decided simply to stand at the crease and propel the ball in the general direction of the batsman. The Tone ducks duly took off, and John bowled two of the batsmen, who were no doubt mesmerised by a combination of the flypast by wild fowl and the unorthodox bowling. In the meantime our tardy car had arrived, its occupants lamely cursing the local one-way system, and normal proceedings were resumed.

It could well have been this same game when we dismissed the Deane for a modest total and reached the same score for the loss of only a couple of wickets, at which point Eric Worrell, the next man in, repaired to the pavilion to get changed. Such over-confidence is always a fatal move and of course the inevitable happened, someone got out and the cry went up "Eric, you're in." We were fearful of some delay, strictly he might even be timed out. The panic was uncalled for, however, for a padless, gloveless and, for all we knew, dangerously boxless figure was already halfway to the wicket, shirt-tail flapping. The next ball from the quick bowler, who had been recalled to the attack, was deftly steered past cover's left hand for four. "I didn't think there was any point hanging about," explained our guileless West Indian.

Over the years many games have been called off or abandoned because of the rain. The opening match of one season was even snowed off, several inches of the white stuff having fallen in the tea interval. This was the first appearance in our ranks of two New Zealanders who had come over for a year and we had quite a lot of difficulty persuading them that this was not typical summer weather. It was also in Taunton that I experienced for the one and only time the abandonment of a game because of too much fine weather. It was during one of the drought years of the seventies, long before global warming became fashionable, and Taunton Outcasts, like so many clubs in the area and in the country as a whole, had been banned from watering their square for weeks. We won the toss and unwisely decided to bat. The first ball from Roy Palmer, who was still playing county cricket, took a huge piece out of the surface on a good length and flew over Chris Harding's head. André Jozwiak at the other end showed an uncharacteristic reluctance to call for a run. The next ball cleared the batsman and the wicketkeeper and the third struck Zorro a painful blow on his helmetless head. The two captains, one of whom was Palmer himself, conferred and commonsense prevailed; the match was curtailed after only these three totally unpredictable balls. We spent the rest of the day unexpectedly sun-bathing.

Places other than Taunton provided some great venues and some exciting encounters: Westlands, home of the helicopters, Street, Morlands of Glastonbury, Frome, Chard and Yeovil, before the land was sold off for housing, to name but a few. It was on a visit to the now defunct Johnson Park, Yeovil, that we were victims of a complete chapter of accidents. We had only reached the Burnt House Inn on the outskirts of Odd Down when part of John Bissex's exhaust system dropped off and John Stevens, selected for one of his first senior games and eager to please, leapt out of the car, picked up the recumbent, detached spare part and, of course, burnt his bowling hand. The nearby pub could have been instantly renamed. The Burnt Bowling Hand Inn might have been a better bet than The Lamplighter which was tried for a bit but couldn't save the hostelry from eventual closure, along with many similar establishments. Yeovil chose to bat and the second ball from Dave Walters flew through off the hard track and struck wicketkeeper 'Spud' Eackett between the eyes causing a gash which necessitated hospital treatment. Dave himself during our innings turned quickly for a second run and badly damaged a cartilage which required surgery later. We lost. On the return journey Dick Millard's big end, whatever that is, something serious, it appeared, went kaput. We all convened in a pub near Shepton Mallet to recover, and Lyn Morgan, whilst carrying a tray of regenerative drinks, tripped over a step and deposited the lot in the lap of John Bell, who had to drive home in his cricket whites. It never rains but it pours, in this instance it poured a mixture of beer and cider.

Hampset, 1973

*Standing (left to right): V. Rosenburg, D. Buckley (who was once in a KES side who were dismissed for one run – a wide), P. Barrett, A. Powell, A. Jozwiak, D. Walters, M. Ball, J. Whitefield
Seated: J. Bissex, M. Johnson, C. Harding, R. Szczotko (doing a passable impression of one of the Pretty Things), K. Tozer (who on one occasion ensured we featured in a genuine tie)*

Playing at the Mendip Hospital in Wells was always an interesting and sometimes a sobering experience. The hospital was the mental asylum, for want of a better term, for quite a wide area. My mother, if we were being a particular nuisance at any time, claimed that we would end up 'sending her to Wells' and we had never quite known what she had meant. The cricket pitch was right in the heart of the establishment, pleasant and beautifully maintained in itself but surrounded by drab, forbidding, grey buildings. On match days, if the weather was at all clement, the inmates were allowed to come out to watch, accompanied by attendant nurses. They always seemed to be uniformly clad in ill-fitting, dowdy clothes, as grey as their surroundings. Our spectators reacted in various, unpredictable ways to the proceedings on the pitch, probably, one felt, without understanding much of what was going on. Some tried to come onto the playing area to join in but had to be restrained. Although we were made very welcome and had some very close games, I was always secretly relieved to leave this particular stop on our varied cricketing journey.

Wherever we went south of Bath we always contrived to stop at Glastonbury on the way back, for the ancient Avalon contained several interesting pubs and, above all, Knights, the best providers of fish and chips in the West Country. A few pints and some of Knights' excellent fare rounded off the day, whether we had won or lost, in the most convivial of ways. The Queen's Jubilee celebrations with dancing in the street, extended licensing hours and general carousing, provided an especially memorable evening of festivities. The extended use of the breathalyser put paid to much of this activity. It is only with a sense of shame that we, upright citizens as we now all are, recall the fact that the drivers made little effort to consume less than anyone else and must have driven around in a state which would now not be tolerated.

Of course we did go in other directions to play. Firstly there were the local sides, Bath, Lansdown and Bath Civil Service. The latter played, when I began, on what has now become Bath University. I had mixed feelings going to this ground as it brought back painful memories of sadistic school cross countries when we were forced to scale the precipitous heights from North Road and then, in a state of near collapse, to stagger around this windswept area. Bring back 'Duster Dowson' and his training runs along the canal, at least it was flat. The Lansdown ground always provided us with a good track and smooth outfield on which to display our skill and, if we could get Les Angell out, we often did quite well. Personally though, I took greatest pleasure from playing at North Parade, home of Bath Cricket Club. Here, sunk in a little bowl close to the river, which in those days before a series of flood prevention schemes which were actually aimed more at preventing people from having to go shopping in Southgate Street in flat-bottomed boats, quite often rose too far and dumped unwelcome sludge and silt on the square, we were right in the heart of the city and yet in a haven of tranquillity.

Two or three of us were once sitting near the entrance from North Parade watching our team-mates bat when we were joined by a curious American and his wife. "Gee

Myrtle, this is just like ballet," enthused the Yank in his variegated Hawaiian shirt. "These extra guys (pointing to the fielders) move in, the pitcher fellow hurls the ball at the striker, he misses, the extras move out again and they start all over again." "I like the costumes, Hiram," intoned Myrtle, rather lasciviously, I thought at the time.

Hampset v Bath, artistically taken through the window of the scorebox or pavilion both of which were then still on the North Parade side of the ground. The Dolemeads and railway side has yet to be developed. What is now the lucrative car park, although still a grassy area, has started attracting rather splendid looking automobiles.

Probably because we were used to the smallness of our Bloomfield Rise home, we found the Wiltshire grounds, such as Trowbridge, Devizes, Chippenham, Westbury and Swindon British Rail, rather large and impersonal, although they had excellent facilities. In the earliest days of my career the Swindon BR team, all of whom were, I think, still railwaymen, came to us by train, no doubt availing themselves of their main perk, free train travel. If we went there on a Saturday, after the match we could join the railwaymen and their families as they let their hair down at a dance in the pavilion which doubled up as the BR Social Club. It was also the only place where, after our exertions on the field, we all cleansed ourselves in a sunken, communal bath tub, which was lined with tiles stamped with the British Railways logo. We were certainly able to 'let the train take the strain', as Jimmy Saville was advising us at the time.

Once in a blue moon we had to go across the Severn to play but I cannot say I particularly enjoyed the experience. I have nothing against the Welsh but why do they moan so much? I don't think I ever met a Welsh batsman who was simply dismissed because the bowler for once proved too good for him. The conditions, the pitch, a crucial distraction and most of all the umpire, who was usually accused in their inimitable lilting way of being a self-abuser, were always to blame, either singly or more often in some conspiratorially concerted way. We also had to cross the bridge, although it is not in Wales, to get to Bream in the Forest of Dean. In pre-league days we were left one Saturday in high season without a fixture and Pete Winch, the fixture secretary at the time, advertised in various local publications for anyone looking for a game. We received one reply, from Bream, but only if we would go to them. The invitation was accepted and we set off, arriving in good time for a 2.30 start. The ground was eerily silent and deserted. By 2.25 we were beginning to believe that there had been a mix-up. Perhaps wires had got crossed and they had journeyed to Bath. We were just about to drive back home when the home eleven plus scorer and umpire to a man all issued forth from the pleasant-looking pub opposite. We had no idea what to expect from the wicket or the rather jolly sounding opposition so in the time honoured fashion of indecision we inserted our hosts. We bowled them out for about 50 and knocked off the runs without loss by about 4.30. I hoped against hope they wouldn't suggest a ghastly second round, as sometimes happens in such circumstances, but no, thank goodness the genial captain said he thought tea would be ready. "We have it in the pub," he explained and led the way back to the hostelry.

After tea it was still quite a bit short of opening time. This was well before politicians dreamed up the idea of converting us all to European café culture by having the pubs open all day, which succeeded only in promoting binge drinking. But the Bream players thought they might be able to prevail upon the landlord to start serving and he duly obliged. We stayed for a couple of pints and then beat a retreat, using as a rather pathetic excuse the need to get back across the bridge in the light. We left our hosts well ensconced and looking as though they were there for the duration. The village pub is rightly often the centre of communal life but this was taking loyalty to one's local to an extreme.

The fact that I am able to say so often, "I've played cricket there" in places far afield in the service of my one club is due to the fact that for many seasons we went 'on tour', spending a week in a different part of the country and playing a match on each of the five days. With the tour sandwiched between the two days of each weekend one could end up playing for eight or nine days on the trot. Tiring but great fun. A spin bowler, who after all in most people's eyes took very little out of himself, was often required to play on every occasion and, as the week wore on and over-indulgence in every sense took its toll, to do more and more of the bowling. On one epic Friday, when we had unwisely agreed to an all-day game, I was required to send down 34 overs and everyone wondered why I was a little jaded when we resumed normal fixtures the next day. Because of increased leisure time now one might expect the annual tour to be even more popular but in fact the opposite seems to be the case. For much of the time I was playing, 'going on tour' was an essential feature of the season for most clubs.

My first experience of touring came when I was about 15 and had barely started playing senior cricket. The destination was the Thames Valley, where we were based in Henley, more precisely in the Catherine Wheel, which is today, I believe, a JD Wetherspoon establishment and, therefore, I imagine, a fairly generic place of plastic uniformity. Then it was a rather charming hostelry of individual character. We played in such towns as Taplow, Marlow, Egham and Henley itself. I can remember nothing of the games except that I have a vague impression that we held our own but usually came off second best. I was immensely proud of appearing with a cross section of the club's members, along with three or four of my contemporaries, although, if truth be told, we were probably there to make up the numbers. Mornings were spent on the river in a variety of crafts, some motorised and some requiring rowing skills which we patently did not have, since our boats seemed to spend a considerable amount of our hiring time going round and round in uncontrolled circles. In the evenings, once we had socialised with each day's hosts and then dined, which for our group of youngsters usually meant in the street outside the local 'chippy', the touring party would repair to the Lounge Bar of the Catherine Wheel to while away a few hours before retiring. It was here that a hierarchical system worthy of the most entrenched medieval society was established. The aristocracy, consisting of the most senior members such as Ken Saunders, Frank Howes and Ron Day, sat in one corner playing bridge with demure concentration, whilst in another section of the bar a middle-ranking set of worthy fellows, led by 'Rosey', who had accompanied the party as umpire, indulged in solo whist. Finally, in a dark recess of the bar skulked a disreputable rabble of reprobates openly gambling for pennies at pontoon. The latter would probably not have been tolerated at all if the public bar had been open but the Lounge was the only area available to non-residents once normal closing time had been reached and last orders had been called. At first we allied ourselves with the pontoon playing serfs, but later in the week 'Rosey' took upon himself a crusading role and endeavoured to instruct us in the rules and subtleties of solo whist with a certain missionary fervour, an educational undertaking he was to continue on winter evenings in the clubhouse in the following close season. We actually got quite good at it.

We also felt extremely adult to be allowed to partake of a couple of glasses per evening of Mann's Brown Ale, the standard brew of the day for the initiation of young men in the pleasures of drinking beer. A few years ago I tried again a similar concoction and I do not think I have tasted anything quite so disgustingly sweet but, at the time, to imbibe in this way seemed to us to be the height of virile sophistication. Not quite binge-drinking but daring all the same. It was also the one and only occasion when I saw alcohol pass Rosey's lips. On the first evening we were astounded to hear him ask, on being offered a beverage, not for the usual 'Stone's Ginger', but for a Dubonnet. After all, if it was good enough for the Monarch's redoubtable mother, why not also for this arch Republican? His ordering of this French tipple was, nonetheless, greeted by a few seconds of amazed silence, even from the pontoon crew.

From left to right: Dave Walters, Ken Saunders and 'Rosey' inspect the latest addition to the Bush Hotel, Farnham, base for the 1958 tour. Perhaps Dave is explaining how it works to his two sceptical looking colleagues.

For the next few years we were unable to pursue any interest in touring for no weeks away were organised, but in 1972 we resurrected the tradition in Hampshire. I was by this time teaching at Taunton's School, or perhaps it had already metamorphosed into Richard Taunton College, in Southampton and I managed to arrange some fixtures. One was against the school itself and here we came up against the burgeoning talent of Tim Tremlett, son of Maurice of Somerset and England fame, and who himself went on to forge an illustrious career with Hampshire, both as a player and an administrator and whose son went on to follow in his grandfather's footsteps and play for England. In view of the club's origins as an amalgam of Somerset and Hampshire, it was a very appropriate encounter. Some recent old boys of the school had also just founded a club which they had rather strangely named 'Krakatoa', perhaps in the hope that they would erupt onto the cricketing scene. In the first year of our Hampshire touring we played against this new outfit on a very sporty wicket in a Southampton park. The fact that the ball consistently flew past our helmetless heads led Sam Shearn to wonder if 'Crack-a-chin-a' might be a more suitable name for our newly formed opposition but we did at least manage to win a low-scoring encounter.

In subsequent years we pushed further out into Hampshire, and even crossed the border into Surrey, to pit our strength against Haslemere, thus renewing an encounter from earlier in the club's history. In both counties we ended up playing against more established clubs mostly on excellent grounds.

For several seasons at that time Hursley Park were having some success in the Village Knock-Out Competition and we enjoyed several visits to their ground and some tense encounters. One year, I seem to remember, they used us as warm-up opposition for the forthcoming final at Lord's. Against St Cross and The Green Jackets we were lucky enough to play in the lovely Winchester water meadows so beloved of Keats, though I am not sure it is recorded how many runs he scored there. Too busy composing odes, one assumes.

On one occasion we travelled west to Lyndhurst in the New Forest to perform on a ground of amazing contrasts. The square was fenced off against wandering sheep, ponies and cattle and a substantial metal structure had to be removed before we could start but the precautions were most effective since the wicket was excellent. The outfield, however, was an undulating mass of gorse bushes and tufty grass liberally sprinkled with the droppings of animals which traditionally roam the forest and this made fielding a memorable experience. It was here that, under the effects of a little too enthusiastic acquaintance with Marston's Pedigree at lunchtime, Stan Szczotko managed to impale himself on a bed of thorns which harboured a liberal amount of animal excreta – and he wasn't even playing on this occasion! At a given moment after tea play had to be suspended while a droverless herd of cows wended their inexorable way to be milked in a diagonal line from deep extra cover across to deep square leg and beyond. The game must have been over before they made the return journey because they never reappeared.

'Crossword Corner' in action at St Cross.
Sun-worshipper Pete Mines, the author and a rather hirsute Reg Trim.
Over many years this trio attempted countless crosswords but completed very few. To the left is Peter Carr, then Secretary of the Club, looking a little somnolent after partaking of several glasses of Gales Ales with lunch. The alert Frank Mines is on duty in the scorebox. Out of shot to the left is Joe Barrett, who had tried to keep up with the other two and, as a consequence, had fallen asleep in a bed of nettles.

Energetic morning activities before afternoon cricketing ones are always an essential part of touring. Here the author and Bill Barrett row in circles around the lake in Petersfield, our base for many of the Hampshire tours.

Hindsight always seems to filter out any less enjoyable moments and I can only ever remember it raining once during our Hampshire odysseys. Shortly after we started on our only trip to Alverstoke a thick, clinging drizzle descended to blot out completely our view of the nearby Solent and put a stop to any ideas we might have had of play. In contrast the sun always seemed to shine when we visited the pleasant ground at Liss and even more so at my favourite venue of all, Tichborne Park. Can it really be that every game we had here ended in a marvellously tense finale, the whole match having been played out under a cloudless blue sky on an idyllic summer's day? Logic would suggest not but that's what it seems like from the standpoint of some forty years on. Nor did the pleasure end with the match, for there was still a convivial evening to look forward to with our hosts in the Tichborne Arms. On one memorable occasion our presence there coincided with a visit from the Bishop of Winchester who was on a pastoral tour of the pubs in his see. What better way to minister to his flock? He even took time out from testing the local God-given ale to bless 'Spud' Eackett and Billy Hallett who had somehow managed to get included in the ecclesiastical round. It must have worked for Billy hit a six next day at Liss, an event as miraculous as turning water into real ale.

All good things come to an end, however, which sounds as if it could be the theme for a sermon from Billy's mentor. It became increasingly difficult to arrange well matched fixtures in the Hampshire area and so we turned our attentions northwards. New Brighton from Merseyside had been visitors to Bloomfield Rise on tour for several years, we had enjoyed evenly fought encounters on the field and had cemented lasting friendships with many of their members. Our friends from the Wirral were always trying to get us to go to them and we started seriously to think of accepting the invitation. Mike Bissex had just ended his county career with Gloucestershire and had gone to play in the Lancashire League and said he could get us fixtures in the Manchester area. And so the new tour was arranged.

To say that we found the first year a challenging experience is something of an understatement. The first match was against Denton, where Mike was the pro. Joel Garner, who was fulfilling a similar role at a club down the road, turned up just before we started but fortunately he had only come to see someone. Phew! No need to worry. Denton batted first and amassed a huge total against a rather makeshift attack. We were beginning to get an idea of what Lancashire League cricket was like. Fortunately Mike was the captain of the Mancunian side and was able to orchestrate a reasonable reply from us by deploying a few part-time bowlers and our blushes were spared.

No such quarter was given the next day, however. At Walkden we were definitely on our own. We turned up and were told that they had had a little difficulty getting out a midweek side (presumably they were all hard at work in the mills in their clogs) and that in addition to their own pro, the current Pakistani Test player Mudassar Nazar, they had drafted in his mate and fellow professional from a neighbouring club, one Pervez Mir, to make up the numbers, along with a lad who opened the bowling for Cheshire. We assimilated this information, which could have been quite flattering, somewhat apprehensively; in fact, our captain for the day retired to the toilets for a while. We lost the toss and were duly asked to field. Mudassar opened the batting and ominously began to stroke the ball at will around the ground, as one might expect from a batsman of his pedigree but, when in about the mid-thirties, he tried to take liberties with the last ball of a John Bissex over, hoisted it towards square leg where Sam Shearn, sprinting round the boundary, took a great catch, low to the ground. Relief all round. It should all be plain sailing from now on. In strode the next mercenary and I had just been introduced to the attack. In line with the by now well-established procedure my first ball to Pervez was a reasonable, orthodox slow left-arm delivery but it was dispatched contemptuously for six straight over long-off. Somewhat taken aback I determined to try to bowl an identical delivery but to hold it back fractionally to induce a false shot and subsequently a catch. The theory worked like a dream, Pervez swallowed the bait and mishit the ball, hard but straight back at me. "Never drop catches off your own bowling," had been one of Ken Saunders's watchwords, a precept I tried to live up to, but on this occasion I could not follow my mentor's advice and a relatively easy catch went embarrassingly to ground. I have dropped some memorable catches in my time but never, I believe, with consequences as serious as this one, for this missed chance has come to haunt me ever since, as the day's ringer, our Pakistani tormentor, proceeded to hit 173 in next to no time. This was no small ground but balls sailed miles out of it on numerous occasions. One thundered onto the top of a car parked miles downwind and disturbed the afternoon activities of a local courting couple. Work came to a standstill on a local construction site so that the builders could witness the massacre from a grandstand view atop their scaffolding. At one stage a friendly Lancastrian bricklayer offered us a hod as a possible aid to swallow any half-chance which might come our way. None did, however, and Walkden posted a formidable total.

At tea we were not too downhearted after the day before, for surely they would use their bowlers imaginatively to give us a chance to score a few runs. However, we had reckoned without northern competitiveness. The lad from Cheshire produced a lively, parsimonious spell and the rest of the bowling was done by Pervez and Mudassar. At Test level the latter was a change bowler but he moved the ball considerably and was too good for most of us. Cue André Jozwiak, for this was the sort of situation in which he revelled and he set about defying the bowling with all the skill and eccentricity at his disposal. Playing out of his crease, twirling his bat, using the back of his bat, even at one stage facing them with the bat upside down, he completely exasperated the professional duo but they did not get him out. Just to complete my day I was the last one to succumb, unable to stay with Joz, largely due to whose efforts we had managed 150, still well short but at least respectable. Several of the opposition players, presumably after having taken an afternoon off work, had contributed nothing to the match but seemed perfectly happy in the bar afterwards as we consumed our pie and mushy peas together for after all their side had won. This was an attitude we found somewhat hard to fathom but which, we assumed, could be put down to a clash of cultures, part of the so-called South/North divide.

A couple of similar matches followed which we lost, but not abjectly at least. At Stalybridge, for example, the home side's opening attack peppered us all afternoon with short-pitched deliveries on a green wicket and thoroughly enjoyed our discomfort. Just think, we had contemplated getting Micky Bissex to turn out for us but, before journeying north, we had rejected the idea as not quite the done thing from the fair play point of view. Naïve southerners or what? For the last encounter of the week we beat a retreat to our friends in New Brighton, there to enjoy a more relaxed, even encounter with familiar faces. We poured out our woes on the chastening experience of our week's touring to our New Brighton colleagues and they promised to get us some fixtures on the Wirral with sides of a similar standard to our own. I am glad that the first year's experiences had not put us off the area entirely for there followed four or five years of what, from the cricketing and all other points of view, turned out to be the most enjoyable of all the tours I took part in. We were already well known at New Brighton and we were quickly made very welcome at Wallasey, Upton and Neston, a club well-known for its hockey section, and we had some excellent games against these clubs in the following years.

The afternoons and evenings were, as usual, taken up by the cricket and after-match celebrations but for the mornings the Wirral offered some interesting possibilities. Of course the area is renowned for golf and there were ample facilities for a round or two on the public links for the proficient and the more inept. This probably convinced me for ever that this was not a game for me. I could hit the little white ball off the tee quite well, although it did seem always to swerve to one side or another towards the end of its trajectory, landing most often in some inhospitable terrain. Furthermore, once on the green, I could putt reasonably accurately but it was the bit in the middle which I could not fathom at all. Even more exasperating were our attempts to indulge in a singularly northern activity – crown bowls. On New Brighton front there was a municipal crown bowling green and on several occasions we did our best to master what looked like a relatively simple pastime. After all, to one side of New Brighton Cricket Club's ground there was a similar facility and time and again we had watched elderly, flat-capped gentleman getting their woods within a cat's whisker of the jack. Surely we, with our keen eye for a ball and with youth on our side, could not fail to do likewise. The green itself looked pretty flat actually so what, we wondered, was all the fuss about? However, even the jack seemed to be biased and it, along with all our woods flew off in directions altogether different to those intended. I do not think anyone in our group ever managed to gain mastery over these wayward spheres on their convex home territory.

On one memorable morning we thought we would desert any sort of sporting venue and take a trip over to Liverpool and perhaps even indulge in a crossing on the Mersey ferry, recently made famous in song. There was only one problem, we had unwittingly chosen the day after the notorious Toxteth riots. On tour we tended not to keep up with the news and had little idea of the unrest sweeping the city. We had half expected a fairly challenging urban environment but thought it a little excessive to have the streets littered with glass and to be peered at by threatening groups of youths on street corners. We managed to find the Pier Head though and had our trip on the ferry and even managed to understand some of the good-humoured scouse banter we encountered.

New Brighton was itself, and no doubt still is, a place of decidedly faded glory and this was certainly true of the Grand Hotel on the sea front, our base in the first year of the tour, where they managed to produce green scrambled egg for breakfast, much to the consternation of Sam Shearn and others. In subsequent years we decamped to a more modest but homelier pub in Wallasey.

The last of our memorable visits to the Wirral took place in 1982. Further tours have stretched to Cornwall (based in Looe, where Mike Bissex was by now running a pub), to Kent and to North Wales but unfortunately the whole idea of a club 'going on the road' for an annual expedition has become less commonplace.

Touring is of course a two-way process and many clubs from near and far, too many to mention in detail, have enjoyed our hospitality at Bloomfield Rise. Perhaps most notable amongst these were the Cayman Islands who came two or three times and allowed us to consider that we had participated in an international match of test match proportions. They were a strong side but we held our own and provided some competitive encounters. The Cayman Islanders seemed to be a very mixed bunch of many hues but, irrespective of colour, they all spoke with that wonderful West Indian lilt, which seems so utterly intended for a cricketing venue and occasion. Perhaps because they had come such a long way, the encounters were always all-day affairs and Fred Narain and his ladies provided a sumptuous lunch. On one of these occasions I was sitting at a table with a couple of the opposition and Graham 'H' Hull, our opening bowler. To make conversation, one of our guests enquired of

Graham, "And what do you do for a living, here in Bath?" "Oh, I'm a tax inspector," was the reply. I have never seen the colour drain so fast from a sun-drenched face before or since.

Although I have never played club cricket for anyone else, I did on occasions play in other places. Firstly there was university in Durham. Cricket was partly responsible for my going there. I was called for interview on a Monday morning in the depths of winter, and the obviously sensible thing to do was to go up in a leisurely fashion on the Sunday to be bright and alert for my interview the next morning. However, on that Sunday I had been invited to the indoor nets at the County Ground in Taunton and I did not want to miss the opportunity to be selected for further training and perhaps selection in representative sides. I decided, against all advice, to travel overnight, which was possible in those days. I duly went to the nets and, late in the evening, having left my kit in the Left Luggage Office at Bristol Temple Meads, boarded a train bound for Scotland. This clapped-out convoy clanked its way across country and was due in the north-east in the wee small hours, thus providing quite an adventure for someone who had not previously ventured further north than about Cheltenham but for whom train travel was at least familiar, after so many trainspotting excursions. This was not quite Orient Express romanticism, however. Shortly after the train lumbered out of Bristol, it started to snow and the ancient carriages had only rudimentary heating so it was not the most comfortable of journeys. Even in the silent, snow-flaked dark the heavy industry of the cities of the Midlands and the North was apparent. I remember distinctly, for instance, the train rattling through what seemed like the middle of steel works with their massive glowing furnaces in Rotherham. I was dropped off about 5.30 am on the dark Durham City station, where the snow had by now accumulated to a thickness of a few inches and where the temperature was fairly low, to say the least. I felt tired, mucky and dishevelled, not quite in the right shape for an important interview but could do nothing other than spend the next couple of hours in a somewhat functional waiting room with peeling paint and draughty windows on Durham station. A cheerful, friendly railwayman did appear with a scuttle full of presumably locally hewn coal to bolster the fire for me. At least I assumed from his demeanour that he was friendly for, in exchanges which were to become typical of my first few weeks in the North-East, our mixture of West Country burr and Geordie English did not lead to the most immediately transparent understanding. I made out that he kept calling me pet and claimed he wouldn't want his own bairns to be ganning about in such weather.

The stillness of the night was occasionally punctuated by trains, mostly goods, clattering through in either direction, although, somewhat disturbingly, I could not summon the interest to dash outside to get their numbers. As day dawned over the snowfields, I saw for the first time the amazing sight of Durham Castle and Cathedral silhouetted against a wan winter sky tinged with flecks of red deemed ominous by folklore. "Aye, we've a canny view from here," opined the lifesaving coal carrier. I gathered he approved of his surroundings.

91

Although my appointment was not until 10 o'clock, I decided to venture down into the town in search of sustenance. I located Hatfield College, my eventual destination, found a small café dispensing breakfast, the whole works of course, including unfamiliar items such as black pudding and pease pudding and, having eaten more than my fill for some derisory sum, still with some time to spare, set off to explore the surroundings.

My wanderings took me through some narrow, cobbled streets into the Market Place, a relatively small area into which traffic, including double decker buses, poured from a variety of directions, all controlled by a policeman enthroned in a white box in the centre of the square from which he issued a series of incomprehensible hand signals. Incomprehensible to the uninitiated, that is, for the locals seemed to know exactly what was going on. A number of years after I had left Durham I revisited and found that the whole area had been pedestrianised in a genteel fashion and, looking back, I could not believe that such a volume of traffic had once clogged this narrow space. A bridge took me over the river and I proceeded past the County Hotel on whose balcony I remembered having seen pictures of fiery, socialist MPs addressing flat-capped crowds at the annual Durham Miners' Gala. I wandered through the forecourt of an austere-looking building which turned out to be Durham gaol, home at Her Majesty's pleasure to some fairly notorious inmates. It was shortly after that I happened on a place which definitely confirmed my growing fascination with the city and my desire to study there – the Racecourse, headquarters of the University Cricket Club and later to be the first county ground for Durham when they became a first class county and before the move to the ground at Chester-le-Street in the shadow of Lumley Castle. There was snow on the ground but, looking down the road, I could make out the traditional wooden cricket pavilion, the roped-off square and the Wear gently rolling past the far side of the ground behind a white, wooden fence. All this lay beneath the imposing outline of the Cathedral, a little way behind me in the distance, and it immediately struck me as a wonderful place to play cricket and so I retraced my steps to Hatfield College, determined to do as well as possible in my interview. These were still the days when one had to gain entry into the College first and the Faculty later. As a preamble and, no doubt, just as a way of initiating conversation, the benign looking Senior Tutor enquired whether I had spent a comfortable night in the College, knowing full well that I hailed from the West Country. On being told that I had come up overnight arriving before dawn, he looked at me pityingly, as if faced with some complete idiot. "Why?" was his bemused reaction. "Because I had to go to the County nets," I replied. He perhaps thought this was some reference to fishing, certainly he did not look particularly impressed. I came to know later that, had I revealed a similar dedication to rugby, I would have been in like a shot without further ado, for these were the days when Hatfield filled its ranks with rugby players to ensure success in the inter-college competition and to provide the University with a powerful side. At one stage during my time there the College itself, let alone the University, had an all-international back row. This led to some ridiculously one-sided encounters with other colleges such as the much smaller St Chad's, then an ecclesiastical establishment whose raison d'être was to produce Church of England ministers and eventual canons, not cannon fodder for rampaging rugby teams.

Hatfield's obsession with rugby meant that Peter Hain and his fellow anti-apartheid campaigners, who came on one occasion to try to persuade the College not to take part in a match against some touring South Africans, achieved little success with their arguments. A debate was held in the Junior Common Room. People listened politely but were determined to go ahead with the match. There was a particularly impassioned plea from a coloured South African the protesters had brought along. I was among the relatively few people in the room who were vaguely sympathetic to their cause but to our shame we kept quiet.

After an inauspicious start, the rest of the interview must have gone quite well for I was accepted and began my university career in the following October, looking forward to perfecting my knowledge of French and German but more, it has to be admitted, to playing on the Racecourse, which had so impressed me on that cold, winter's morning.

This was just a little before Durham University Cricket Club entered a golden era during which it produced a string of county and test players, including at least two future England captains. On the other hand it was some time after the days of Frank Tyson who had played and studied there, a fact commemorated in the pavilion by a stump, shattered by the ' typhoon' during his student days, which was hung above the opposition's dressing room door, a timely reminder perhaps of what they were likely to face.

My first year at Durham in the University side, in my normal position for team photographs, far right on the back row.

In my time at Durham we could not quite match such feats but we had a decent side which consistently played at a good standard against clubs and other university sides. The former, mostly members of the Durham and Northumberland leagues, were quite strong and played on good grounds, though a few were in somewhat indifferent surroundings. At Billingham or Hartlepool, for example, we played on an excellent square and a smooth outfield but the drawback was that it was in the middle of a petro-chemical plant which gave off a noxious odour which made Bridgwater with its cellophane works smell like the most fragrant of roses. One Sunday during my time in Durham, representative sides drawn from each of the county leagues played against each other on the Racecourse and I recall it turned into a sort of boxing match between two great West Indian cricketers, Rohan Kanhai and Lance Gibbs, who were both plying their trade in the area at the time. I think Lance Gibbs, who took eight wickets, won but not before his compatriot had scored a flowing century.

Mid-week we either played against other universities or some sundry opposition. Amongst the latter were the Royal Signals Regiment who annually escaped from Catterick to play us and provided a wonderful example of hierarchical organisation. They were invariably skippered by an officer, usually with about the rank of a captain. He was joined by a couple of lower-ranking staff officers. This trio would bat four, five and six, might turn in the odd over of ineffectual spin bowling and would field close to the bat or at mid-on and mid-off, rarely catching anything and making little effort to cut off any balls which passed even a slight distance to right or left of them. Such mundane tasks were done by other ranks but usually with an NCO acting as intermediary. If a ball was dispatched some way over the boundary, perhaps down towards the river and some idle students punting or rowing there or lazing on the banks with an unopened book and a picnic, a conversation which seemed strange to the non-military would ensue. " Better have the ball sent back, Jenkins." "Wilco, Sir. Sergeant-Major, get the ball sent back, will you?" "Right you are Sir." "Oy, you, Private Smith/Jones/Bloggs, get that ……….. ball back from those layabouts over there."

 Privates Smith/Jones/Bloggs and perhaps a couple of Lance Corporals and Corporals, as well as doing all the fetching and carrying in the field also had to open the batting, just to see off any hostile bowling, and particularly had to do the majority of the bowling. They also only batted at the end, if required. This made the team unpredictable as an opposition batting force for often these other ranks were very competent, if given a chance. You could easily reduce the Signallers to about 60 for five, only to find their best batsmen coming in at the end. Later in the Dun Cow, a wonderful pub opposite the gaol, to which we always repaired after matches, the same organisation would obtain. The officers never handled any money. The kitty would be held by someone of about Sergeant rank. "Get another round in, will you, Sergeant? Same again for us, make sure the student lads are OK. Oh and (to give the Captain his due) make sure Smith/Jones/Bloggs et al have got a pint. By the way, have they stowed the kit? See to it, will you?" The one of lowly rank most to be pitied, however, was the driver, probably someone on jankers for some misdemeanour, who had to sit around outside in his Army mini-bus, waiting on the whims of his superiors for a signal to break camp and transport them back to base.

The most eagerly awaited games, however, were against rival universities, particularly in the keenly contested UAU competition. Durham, of course, played in the north-east section along with Newcastle, Hull, York and Sheffield. The winners of this section always went on to play against the winners of the north-west equivalent league. During my four years of playing for the university we only managed this on one occasion. This was almost entirely due to the fact that for most of this time Sheffield had in their ranks Frank Hayes, who was to go on to great things with Lancashire and England, and also an old acquaintance of mine, Bob Clapp of Somerset and Burnham. Between them these two usually ensured that Sheffield made good progress in the competition. In the year we did make it through to the knock-out phase we travelled to play Liverpool University in a two-day encounter. Honours were just about even after the first day but a late night sampling the entertainment delights of the swinging sixties city in general and of the Cavern Club in particular, 'just to see what all the fuss was about', meant that we did not do so well on the following day and made no further progress in the competition.

It was also while I was at Durham that I took part in the most unproductive tour imaginable. In that particular year the Cricket Club Secretary was reading Geography and Meteorology. One might have expected this academic background to counsel against a cricket tour of the Scottish universities in the first week of May but such was not the case and off we set on a grey, drizzly morning. Results of our efforts read as follows: v Edinburgh University – rained off, v St Andrew's University – rained off, v Aberdeen University – snowed off, v Strathclyde University – rained off, v Glasgow University, Durham 84 for four, match abandoned, rain. The tour organiser had also excelled himself on the last night in Glasgow by booking us into a dry hotel run by two elderly spinsters who offered us cocoa and biscuits. Next day we fled south, to Gretna Green and the possibility of getting a drink, but unfortunately not to any improvement in the weather.

If nothing else university gave me the opportunity to play in a lot of different places and the ability to say many years later, 'I've played cricket there.' I was on the Racecourse the day our degree results were announced, my West Country Hatfield friend and fellow linguist Colin Trim had to relay the news that I'd got a First to me at mid-on. The news was overpowering and I immediately dropped a catch. This time I had a slight excuse.

The other experience which took me to yet more playing venues was that of appearing for Somerset Second Eleven. This sounds very grand but in fact was far from it. Between leaving school at Easter in what was then known as the third year sixth and going to Durham I had time to kill. This was a time when Somerset had an extremely small staff and, when the First Eleven was playing and before the University term ended and a few young players became available, they struggled to put out a second string. Anyone with time on their hands stood a good chance of getting in, particularly away from home. They could usually find some decent club cricketers to bolster the professional ranks when a two-day match was held at the County Ground in Taunton but those who needed to take time off work to play were a bit more reluctant to travel far from home and my ready availability for away games was an attraction for the selectors. Thus I only featured in a couple of home games at Taunton, one against Kent and one against Glamorgan, a match in which Dave Walters was also selected.

By playing in a few Second Eleven games in that season between school and university I certainly saw some different parts of the country: Worcestershire at Worcester, Essex at Witham, Sussex at Hove, Leicestershire at Lutterworth. My first game was very early in the season at Worcester. We went there with our usual mix of a handful of fringe professionals who were not in the First Eleven and some willing club cricketers who happened to be available. Unfortunately the home side did not have a county match and, since it was very early season, they took the opportunity to give some practice to some quite big names. Thus we came up against Carter, Standen, Brain, Ormrod, Headley and some chap who was spending a year qualifying called Basil d'Oliviera. When we arrived sitting in an easy chair on the pavilion steps we found Tom Graveney. Fortunately he preferred to stay there doing the crossword in the sun rather than bother taking easy runs off us. D'Oliviera's biographer, in making the point that Basil was a 'big occasion performer', writes that his subject did not actually set the world alight in his qualifying year against sub-standard opposition. With this last phrase he probably had us in mind for the game was obviously a bit of a mis-match, although I can safely say it was the only one in which I was ever involved in defeat by an innings – and plenty to spare! This was the first time I had ever spent virtually the whole day in the field and the next morning in our Worcester hotel I could barely get out of bed, leave alone bowl properly, even if Worcester had had to bat again. The other games were much closer; I learnt a lot and even picked up a few wickets.

In the game against Essex at Witham the home side had in their ranks a certain G. Hurst. In this particular match he did very little, but a couple of years later he completed a memorable hat-trick for England at Wembley.

The organisation and general welfare of the Somerset Second Eleven at the time were in the hands of that wonderful ex-county pro Bill 'The Hand that Bowled Bradman' Andrews. Several times I travelled to away matches with him in his car. At first I thought this was a great honour but later realised that other more streetwise members of the side were doing their best to avoid this nerve-shattering experience. Bill took little notice of other road users but occasionally sought to communicate his own intentions to them through a series of eccentric gestures, all of which involved his ever-present pipe, alight or extinct, being stuck out of the window and being made to describe all sorts of loops and circles. Presumably these strange signals meant something to Bill but they certainly made no sense to anyone else. Whilst driving Bill also indulged in a constant, one-sided conversation, which did not aid his concentration.

SOMERSET II BEATEN

Somerset 2nds were beaten by four wickets by Kent 2nds at Taunton, important roles for the visitors being played by two normal first-teamers, Dave Halfyard and John Prodger.

After Kent, with a first innings lead of four, Somerset reached 92 for the loss of two wickets, but then collapsed against Halfyard, who took 6-35, and were all out for 135.

Kent suffered early shocks and had to fight to win, but a stand between Prodger and Ealham saw them well on their way.

SOMERSET II. (1st innings) 101 for 7 wkts, dec.—Cuckney 5-39, Page 1-35.

Second innings

Robinson lbw b Halfyard	... ...	38
Willetts b Page	... - ...	15
Eele c Ealham b Halfyard	... ...	23
Doughty c Cuckley b Olton ...	...	15
Palmer c Knott b Halfyard ...	...	1
Granville lbw b Olton	...	11
Stockham c Prodger b Halfyard	...	6
Holland c Loader b Halfyard	...	0
L Robinson b Olton	...	3
Johnson not out	...	0
Extras	...	16
Total	...	135

Bowling: Halfyard 6-35.

KENT (1st innings) 105 for 8 wkts, dec.)—Prodger 38, Robinson 4-51, Hall 4-34, Doughty 0-10.

Second innings

Nicholls c Eele b Palmer ...	...	15
Finn c Doughty b Hall	...	9
Ealham b Palmer	...	33
Prodger c Willetts b Doughty	...	53
Knott b Palmer	...	0
Dudgeon c Hall b Johnson ...	...	0
Olton not out	...	12
Halfyard not out	...	0
Extras	...	10
Total (for 6 wkts)	...	132

Bowling: Hall 1-32, Palmer 3-32, Doughty 1-35, Johnson 1-5.

A typical Second Eleven performance. First innings DNB. Second innings 0 not out (probably did not face). One wicket in a short spell in the second innings. My Kentish scalp seems well named for one who failed to trouble the scorers. His mood probably matched his name.

I do not know to what extent Bill was responsible for making all the mundane arrangements associated with away fixtures but they were utterly chaotic. We got lost on virtually every journey. On one occasion, after some considerable time spent driving around Leicestershire, we arrived late at our hotel in Lutterworth. In marched the tall imposing figure of our coach and mentor who announced himself as 'Andrews, Somerset County Cricket Club'. This was met by a look of puzzlement from the receptionist. No bookings had been made, the hotel was completely full and no other accommodation was available in the town. We ended up spending the night in an old folks' home, much to the consternation of the inhabitants who believed their domain was being taken over by a much younger generation. Breakfast consisted of food easily absorbed by those with few teeth. Our stay here could not have done us much harm, though, as it was followed by the only match in which I was involved in my short county career which we actually won.

Although in forty-six years I never played for any other club, cricket took me to many interesting places and venues. The only unproductive year was the one I spent as an 'assistant anglais' in Reims, plenty of champagne but little opportunity to turn my arm over.

Days not so much in the sun

To encapsulate the pleasure he gained from watching and writing about cricket, Neville Cardus entitled one of his collections of literary pieces *Days in the Sun*. Most of the time I spent playing at Hampset and elsewhere were such days in the sun. But not all. It would be naïve to think that in cricket or indeed in life in general there would be no counterbalancing periods of rain.

From a personal point of view the most shattering event came during my year in France. I enjoyed my time there from the beginning of the academic year but by May I was starting to regret not being back home on the cricket field, there being no opportunity to play in the vineyards of Champagne. The last day of the month came, my father's birthday; I had sent a card and was wondering if it had got there in time. A message came from the lycée's reception, someone had been trying to phone me but had not really been able to make themselves understood. The secretary thought they had said they would ring back in an hour, could I be on hand? The call duly came, it was Mr Sheppard, the insurance rep who called regularly on my mother to pick up her penny and twopenny premiums on some policies she had, who lived up the road and had a phone. My father had had a road accident and was in Frenchay hospital, could I come at once? I got permission to leave from the proviseur, and Ernst, the German assistant drove me to Calais in his Volkswagen. I hitched a lift to London from a fellow ferry traveller and got a train to Bath. The whole journey had not taken long but there was nothing I could do. My father had been knocked from his bike whilst coming home from the Combe Down Co-op on his birthday, mown down in the Firs by a Mathesson's cold meats van and was in a coma in hospital in Bristol. The doctors held out little hope that he would come round and, if he did, there was a good chance he would be brain-damaged. Sometimes, they said, singing or reciting a favourite piece of music or poetry brought people round from such a state. It was worth a try. At that time he was particularly fond of *Dominique* by the Singing Nun and, of course, from his days of recuperation on Capri, anything by Gracie Fields. And so for a few days we gathered round the bed and, rather incongruously and no doubt unmelodically, tried rendering *Sally, Sally, pride of our alley* and, although he knew no French, the currently popular ditty from the Belgian sister. Our efforts yielded no reward but it made us feel better. I went back to France to wind up my year there and then returned home for good. Shortly afterwards, a few days before my own 21st birthday in July, my father succumbed. The doctors tried their best to persuade us that it was a blessed release. I had one year left at university. I determined I would do the very best I could.

Tragedies affected us all at Hampset too. Not all can be chronicled but the most dramatic loss remains that of the then club captain, Dave Walters, who collapsed and died during a league match against Taunton Deane in 1986. We had batted first and had made a reasonable total in our allotted overs. I had not been required and Dave himself was in, undefeated at the end of the innings, helping to put on some quick runs in typical fashion in the final few overs.

Dave Walters in his early years at Hampset,
playing billiards in a clubhouse somewhere on tour.

It was off with the pads and straight back out onto the square to supervise the rolling of the wicket and the re-painting of the white lines, such was the lot of the skipper who had to shoulder responsibility for just about everything. Belatedly, therefore, Dave came in to tea for some quick refreshment prior to retaking the field to captain the side and open the bowling. I had already gone back to the dressing room to don boots and sweater, ready for our turn in the field, when someone relayed the news that Dave had gone to the hatch to get his tea and had collapsed. Graham Hull and others tried desperately to dredge out of their memories the by now mostly forgotten elements of first aid courses attended long before. Mike Scaggs's daughter, then a trainee nurse, was hurriedly summoned to bring more professional assistance but Dave's ashen face gave no sign of response. Emsie Walters arrived just before the ambulance but was equally powerless. As the vehicle pulled out of the ground, its siren wailing, through a side window we could see a paramedic desperately working to revive the inert form of our skipper, who minutes earlier had been striking the ball cleanly and running purposefully between the wickets. The game was of course abandoned; the opposition left shocked and soberly murmuring their regrets at what had happened and their hopes for a happy outcome. Words do not come easily in such circumstances.

It was not long before the news we had all been dreading, expecting, hoping against came through: dead on arrival. A period of numbed silence followed; no-one knew quite what to do. We all tried for once to busy ourselves with the trivial but necessary jobs which come at the end of any game, collecting the stumps, putting away the umpires' coats, pushing the sightscreens to one side, sweeping up the damaged ends. On this occasion a couple of tasks were left undone, there were no finishing touches to put to the scorebook and no match report to submit to the league. Slowly in dribs and drabs we gathered up our kit and made our way home after what was surely the worst cricketing day of any of our lives. The usual post-match dialogue with my mother ran somewhat differently: "You're home early, how did you get on?" "Dave Walters dropped dead at tea-time." "Oh, his poor wife and children." And there the conversation stopped.

Someone who had one of the worst jobs on that fateful day was Bill Hallett who was taking part in the reciprocal Second Eleven game away at Taunton Deane. Dave's son, Mike Walters, was playing in the second team that day and it fell to Bill to break the news and escort him back to Bath.

For Emsie Walters, however, the tragedy did not end there. Not long after Dave's premature death I came home one day to Trowbridge after a day at school in West Lavington and stopped off at the newsagents to buy a copy of the *Bath and Wilts Chronicle*, either to read match reports from the previous weekend or to see the teams for the one to come. A pile of *Chronicle*s lay on the counter and, as I waited my turn to purchase a copy, I was suddenly aware of two photos of the youthful Mike and Julie Walters smiling at me from the front page. But this was no happy story, both had been killed in a freak road accident on their way home from work the previous day. 'How much can one woman take?' was my first reaction, as I thought of the accumulated pain that Emsie must have been going through. Years later I received an unexpected e-mail from her from New Zealand where she was living not far from her surviving daughter Sarah and her family. She reported that she was still working for the Social Services (continuing to help others, I thought) and that her two grandsons were shaping up as good cricketers. That would have pleased Dave, had he not left us on that summer's day twenty-five years ago.

There was some debate about whether we could fulfil our fixture the following Saturday against Taunton St. Andrew's but we decided to go ahead. Mike Bissex, one of Dave's greatest friends, came to help us out, otherwise the team was as the previous week. The match, like all Somerset League fixtures that day, was preceded by a period of silence. In spite of our determination to do our best for our missing captain's sake we just could not seem to concentrate. Micky managed about 20 and the rest of us were all out for a paltry 50-odd. We slunk back home thoroughly dispirited. Slowly we recovered and at least retained our First Division status but the events of that day and the subsequent horrors which engulfed the Walters family reverberated for much longer and have surely never been forgotten by those who experienced them first hand.

Less dramatic but more drawn-out, and painful in a different way, was the early death of Mervyn 'Spud' Eackett, a victim of one of the grisly manifestations of cancer. In the last few weeks of his life 'Spud' refused to let anyone but his very closest relatives see him, so ashamed was he of his haggard appearance, the plaything of the ravages of his disease. The desire to slip away unnoticed, unsung, without any fuss was typical of his self-effacing nature. A competent batsman, a tidy, effective wicket-keeper and a brave scrum half, Mervyn had given his whole life to sport and his gnarled fingers and pronounced limp from damaged hips gave visible testimony to his dedication. A quiet courage pervaded his performances as opening bat and wicket-keeper and 'Spud' also served various sides as captain over the years, and to this he brought a quiet, thoughtful authority. Early on in this role for the Second Eleven he often had to endure the intemperate, unintelligent responses of many of his youthful charges but I never saw him become impatient or angry. I still feel acutely embarrassed at the memory of one such response in a game at home to Yeovil. 'Spud' had batted all the way through when I came in to join him still with about 20 minutes to go before tea. "Try to stay in, Blocker and I'll get what I can," was the only instruction. Three balls later I holed out at long-on after a cross-batted heave at an innocuous off-break. "Not quite what I had in mind. We'll have to bowl well," was Mervyn's measured reaction.

Mervyn 'Spud' Eackett, 4th from the left, padded up waiting to bat on tour in 1958.
From left to right: Alan Telford, Brian Horler (a contemporary of Dave Walters, who soon after this went to work on Merseyside and was never seen again), Ken Saunders, 'Spud', Ken Saunders' father, Cyril Butler (not playing this day or confident he would not be needed to bat), John Bell, Ken Hodges (still evergreen five decades later). The sartorial elegance of those in mufti is much to be admired.

'Spud' Eackett also devoted countless hours to club affairs, notably on the square, where he painstakingly produced some of the best wickets seen at Bloomfield Rise over a number of seasons. He had his own method, mapped out by complicated lines of twine held in place by meat skewers, of squeezing the maximum number of playing strips out of the limited resources of a small square. 'Spud' slipped quietly out of our lives towards the end of the eighties but his absence was felt for years to come.

Most thought provoking of all is when someone is taken prematurely from one's own generation and this happened for me and those of a similar age with the early loss of Richard 'Dickie' Densem. As a lad and teenager he was always chirpy, cheerful and good-humoured. He embraced the fashion and music of the sixties with great enthusiasm but also found time to become a very competent cricketer and footballer. He always wanted to be a carpenter and left school at quite a young age to take up an apprenticeship to fulfil this aim. Little did we know that the seeds of his demise were probably sown at this stage. He later became a great craftsman, one of his projects when still in his teens was to build a sightscreen which stood the test of many years. Before this the only aid to a batsman in front of Dotty Shellard's house was a temporary, canvas contraption which was forever flapping in the breeze or blowing over in anything above about three on the Beaufort scale. Single-handed the young nascent carpenter created a structure which withstood gales, tempests and various other batterings over many years.

Whilst an apprentice in days when Health and Safety had never been heard of he was no doubt given dusty, dirty jobs to do with no protection. How could anyone foresee that even then the consequences of such work were to gnaw away at him for years and eventually literally throttle the life out of him. I saw him at Dave Buckley's 25th wedding anniversary in Cheshire and he seemed fine.

It was a great shock to receive a phone call not long after from Reg Trim informing me of Dickie's death. This seemed impossible for he was so full of life. In our teenage years he was the one of all of us who most enthusiastically caught the spirit of the times. Cars fascinated him and this was almost his undoing for at one stage he was involved in a nasty accident in which Barbara, his petite future wife, was badly injured. A dedicated follower of fashion, his kipper ties were broader and gaudier than any others, his trousers flared in the extreme or clung like drainpipes, if the fashion demanded, and his hair was cut in the latest style. This was how I remember him, so what was Reg talking about, how could such a figure possibly be ready for burial? But ready he had been made, as we soberly witnessed a few days later. United at a funeral those of my generation determined to meet more often at reunions of the living. One of Dickie's favourite songs was *All the young dudes* by Mott the Hoople; we had even had the DJ play it especially for him at that wedding anniversary. That will do as my next record, a reminder of all of those dismissed before they had time to blossom at the crease.

Basic skills (i)

The equivalent in cricket of the three Rs in education are the three Bs: batting, bowling and bending down to retrieve a ball which has just trickled through your legs, otherwise known as fielding. The latter activity throws up all sorts of conundrums. Why is it, for example, that on inclement afternoons, when you have already committed a couple of fielding gaffes, the ball seems to follow you around, wherever a long-suffering captain tries to hide you? Why do the last five overs of a league innings, when the opposition has made plenty for very few, seem to take longer to get through than the preceding 40? Why does a momentary lapse in concentration always coincide with a less than competent fieldsman being called into action? For example, Reg Trim, who later became a perfectly respectable fielder, plaintively recounts that his only memory of his first ever game for Hampset, a Second Eleven encounter at Corsham, in which he was required neither to bat nor to bowl, is of dropping a catch at deep square leg when his concentration faltered for a moment whilst he was observing a local maiden extricating herself from a mini-car clad in a ridiculously short mini-skirt. It was the early sixties after all.

It is true that the likes of Colin Bland, Derek Randall and Jonty Rhodes elevated fielding to an art form, that the level of athleticism in the modern professional game is incredibly high and that, even at a lowly level, the advent of club league cricket led to a huge overnight improvement in this cricketing skill, nevertheless it remains a Cinderella activity, something for the Ugly Sisters rather than the leading parts. When does a fielder, for instance, ever lead his team from the arena covered in plaudits, having secured victory for his side? Performing with anything less than perfection in the field often brings opprobrium and ridicule down on the head of the perpetrator from the spectators. A batsman wafting at a wide delivery and failing to make contact by a matter of feet brings no adverse reaction from the crowd, however hostile it might be. Similarly a bowler who produces a series of long-hops, full tosses, wides or no-balls can normally expect to escape censure, he just gets taken off and hopes to retreat to a safe area of the field where he will not be troubled for a bit while he contemplates his own shortcomings. A fielder, however, who fails to cut off a boundary, in spite of hurtling around the edge at full tilt and ending up with a despairing, trouser-staining dive or, even worse, fluffs a chance, however hard it might be, almost inevitably finds his best efforts greeted by ironic cheers, jeers and cat-calls, even from his own supporters. It's just like in a restaurant or canteen when someone drops and breaks something; this is almost always followed by loud cheers. I've never quite understood why.

Fielder baiting can even take place at our level. The whitewashed wall on the far side of Bath Cricket Club which separates the ground from the Dolemeads used to be a class boundary in the days when the wooden pavilion with its steep steps up to the changing quarters was safely situated on the city side of the playing area. Beyond the wall lay a scrofulous den of low-life populated by fallen women, crooks and idlers. From the opposite perspective on the other side of the same wall was to be found a frivolous area on which the toffs and the idle rich in general could be seen at play. Occasionally the inhabitants of the Dolemeads would express their resentment and their seething sense of injustice by pouring scorn on the cricketing gentry in the field which abutted their abodes. A line of unkempt, unwashed heads would appear over the top of the stonework and yell foul-mouthed insults at the world in general and any fielders who happened to be in close proximity. If anyone, perhaps unnerved by the barracking, committed a fielding error or dropped a dolly, this was grist to the mill for the amused onlookers. The sensible thing to do was to ensure that you were fielding well away from the source of this ribaldry. Those who knew what to expect would follow closely on the heels of the captain down the well-trodden, wooden steps of the pavilion and immediately volunteer to take third man on the North Parade boundary, thus ensuring that they displayed their fielding prowess, or more likely lack of it, in front of a more genteel, indulgent audience of middle-class city dwellers and well-heeled tourists.

The invective which was sometimes heaped on fielders in front of the Dolemeads, however, was nothing compared to that which was commonly experienced for a few years at Devizes. Led by a certain Dicky Mullins, a group of uncouth locals would gather on match days at Devizes Town FC in winter and at Devizes Cricket Club in summer to witness the events and pour scorn on the sporting endeavours of those playing. The group was made up mostly of dustmen; no doubt their more recent counterparts have become known as refuse collectors, re-cycling facilitators and by other even more fanciful terms but then they were dustmen. As a way of relaxing after a week spent humping metal trash cans around the Wiltshire market town, they spent summer weekend afternoons at the cricket, drinking copious quantities of bottled beer and playing cards for money. They would break from such nefarious activities, which were probably illegal, if there was even a hint of a fielding weakness and subject the unfortunate player involved to a tirade of merciless criticism. "Get theeself a bucket lad," would shout Dicky et al, "you couldn't catch a cold." " Where did they get you from, you lanky streak of piss, my granny could do better." " Yeah, an' she's pushin' up daisies, ain't she, Dicky?" "No wonder you let that through yer legs, ya poofter, ther's plenty o' room." It was just possible to placate them a little by wandering around the ground during one's own side's innings, by expressing untold pleasure at renewing acquaintance with them after another year and, above all, by offering them large numbers of Woodbines. Such ingratiating behaviour, however, rarely had any lasting effect, the next dropped catch was greeted with guffaws of laughter and the same acerbic repartee. And then one year they were simply not there any more. It was rumoured that the police had caught up with them but they had probably just moved on to plague the life out of dancers, huntsmen, cyclists, rowers or some other group intent on innocent pleasure. Visits to Devizes were never quite the same; somehow we missed Dicky and his henchmen, a bit in the same way that you eventually miss a wart which has suddenly disappeared.

On a fine summer's afternoon, when you successfully avoid much contact with the ball, fielding can be a reasonably pleasant way of spending a couple of hours or so, particularly if the surroundings are picturesque or congenial, but in general it is an activity in which you must aim for as much damage limitation as possible. Positions are all important and it is best to try to monopolise the combination which is the least demanding for the athletically challenged: third man at one end and mid-on at the other. I came to this conclusion very early on through watching Somerset with Horace Hazell, who was a fine, West Country slow left-armer but was also one of the most indifferent professional fielders ever seen. The trick is to work out immediately on arrival at any ground which end will give you the least throwing distance and, on taking the field, to make your way resolutely to third man or mid-on at that end, depending on where the opening over is to come from, before anyone else can usurp the position which is rightfully yours as the side's worst fielder. At Hampset this of course means the pavilion end. Third man is a very congenial place to put oneself, for, stationed on the boundary, there are usually a few people with whom one can converse. Even on a ground as small as Hampset's, catches, even from the wildest of swings, are rarely likely to reach you and, if they do, they are so out of the blue that you cannot reasonably be expected to take them. The batsman does not usually hit the ball directly at third man, most often you merely have to deal with a thick edge which comes at you at a manageable speed. The only real thing to avoid is the embarrassing four through the legs, the ball trickling over the boundary in an awkward silence "Sorry Skip, hit a bump/divot/rabbit hole" (which only you can see) is not usually a convincing explanation.

At mid-on the ball can be hit a bit more deliberately at you but at least the majority of batsmen are more adept at hitting straight with venom on the off side than on the leg. There is no way round it, you have to make a reasonable fist of standing at mid-on, since a consistent display of incompetence here can lead to the indignity of being posted at third man at both ends, which, if nothing else, is extremely tiring. In the face of a ferocious onslaught from an opposing batsman you can find yourself asked to retreat to long-on and it is on these occasions that you hope that the big-hitter either clears you with something to spare or that he becomes more agricultural and begins to favour deep mid-wicket for his aerial bombardment. If, as a bowler, you can manage to be kept on for a fairly long spell, you can avoid being at mid-on too much, escaping to third man between overs. For a seasoned campaigner this is a crucial factor when deciding the end from which you prefer to operate.

The tactical importance of laying claim to the shortest boundary cannot be stressed enough for those whose throwing capacity is restricted. An astute batsman on the other side will soon become aware of such a limitation and the loud call which echoes around the ground of "Come two, he can't throw" is to be avoided if at all possible, even in those fortunate souls who are the most insensitive to criticism. The fading ability to throw a cricket ball any respectable distance is akin to the worst cases of virility loss and anyone who could invent some form of Viagra which delayed this loss of manliness would surely make a fortune. Only for a very short spell, from about the age of seventeen to my early twenties, could I really throw. On most grounds I was able to throw hard, reaching the wicketkeeper with a flat, fast trajectory and sparing him the need to leap high and wide or grovel in the dust to try to avoid overthrows. I must admit that the thwack into the gloves certainly was a most satisfying sound. If such a throw resulted in a run-out the pleasure was even greater, but it didn't last. Somewhere along the line, probably over-exerting myself in an attempt to show off, I 'threw my arm out', whatever that means, and it was never the same again. With age, and I was not the only one to suffer in this way, throws became ever more feeble and the distance covered ever shorter until towards the end I had to resort to a whirling, over-arm action which got the ball somewhere near the square but the high, looping flight allowed the slowest of batsmen to take liberties and to make his ground comfortably.

In certain circumstances two fielders go for the same ball and the athletically challenged fielder has a couple of options. The most obvious thing to do is to contrive that one's colleague reaches the ball first. This is not always possible without seeming almost to go backward, so one can sometimes attempt a sort of music-hall act in which one flips the ball nonchalantly to a team-mate with a better arm. I tried this a few times but once I succeeded only in sending the ball over the boundary instead of into the safe hands of a following fielder, so I gave up.

Ground fielding of course has its pitfalls, literally sometimes, but catching is even more problematic. Failing to take extremely hard half chances on a freezing cold day can be easily excused, but dropping absolute dollies is more difficult to explain away, the sun being in one's eyes will evidently only serve in certain meteorological conditions. What makes things worse is if the reprieved batsman goes on to make a big score. Pervez Mir from 6 to 173 has been chronicled elsewhere. An almost equally embarrassing moment occurred much earlier when Graham 'Budgie' Burgess lived to fight another day to everyone's cost. We were playing Morlands Glastonbury and 'Budgie' was just starting out on a long and successful county career. He was showing great promise for the Glastonbury side and we knew we would have to get him early if they were not to post a big total. After only a few balls he eyed the short Hampset boundary and attempted a lofted drive straight down long-on's throat, the said fielder having been moved back expressly for this purpose. Straight in, straight out, huge total to face. We do not get very close. Long-on and everyone else feel glum.

Actually taking catches, which is bound to happen now and then by the law of averages, can be quite fortuitous. I can remember hurtling around the boundary – well, perhaps chugging would be a better word – in an attempt to get near a 'skier' in one of our international encounters with the Cayman Islands, sticking out a forlorn hand and the ball stuck. In such circumstances it is best to affect a nonchalant air, as if the whole manœuvre had been totally planned, throw the ball back in as matter-of-fact way as possible, as if the only thing of any importance is to get on with the next ball. In the meantime one's team-mates are probably falling about in disbelief. If you can manage to take a spectacular catch off your own bowling – I have one isolated instance in mind when at Shirehampton I took off and clasped a hard return inches from the ground in a most uncharacteristic display of acrobatics – it is best to adopt a world-weary countenance as if the whole battle with the opposition is falling on your broad, philanthropic shoulders.

In my last season we were involved in a very tight finish at Timsbury and in such circumstances the poor captain can sometimes lose his grip on the situation. Somehow in the penultimate over, probably it was something to do with the 'four in the circle' rule, I found myself brought up from third man to field just backward of cover point – unheard of. What's more, again because of some miscalculation in the bowlers' allotment, we were forced to turn to part-time bowler Paul Collard. To compound the situation the batsman was facing who had been mostly responsible for guiding the home side to within a few runs of our total. Prospects looked bleak. The first ball was sent unceremoniously for four. The second was smote off the back foot straight at the makeshift cover point who somehow managed to parry the ball high in the air which made it fairly easy to 'pouch' safely. More need for nonchalant pretence that all had been planned in advance. I don't know if anyone collects unusual scorebook entries but 'Unfortunate batsman caught Johnson bowled Collard' must be a real collector's item.

Catches and particularly failed attempts to accept them can be physically and morally damaging. In my case the most spectacular example occurred at Bath when their opening bat, Rodney Summers, smashed the ball straight back at me about head high. I tried to make my efforts to shield myself look like an endeavour to take the catch but succeeded only in breaking two fingers. As this was the most serious injury I sustained in 47 years playing, I can't really complain, except that the pain still lingers in the form of an arthritic, difficult to bend middle finger, an everlasting reminder of ineptitude.

I have noticed recently that younger members of our sides, no doubt aping what they see professionals do on the television, have taken to making sliding stops just inside the boundary. If executed properly this looks a most impressive piece of co-ordinated movement and of course it saves one or two runs. I thought I ought to give it a go at least and the opportunity presented itself one day at Lansdown, of all places, as I chased the ball towards the pavilion boundary. I thought I could slide and in one movement scoop the ball backwards without disturbing the boundary rope. It all seemed to be going quite well but unfortunately I missed the ball and ended up in a flower bed, entwined in a low link fence. An obliging local terrier retrieved the ball for me. From then on allowing the ball to cross the boundary seemed a much better, more dignified option, although a series of long-suffering bowlers probably did not share this view.

I was fortunate over the years to witness from my posts at third man and long-on or, more importantly from the end of my bowling follow-through, fielding which was several degrees more competent than my own. Dave Walters would catch most things at slip, as would André Jozwiak at long-on. Murray Day, who had been a promising gymnast at school, took some amazingly acrobatic catches off my bowling at extra cover. I think I would have to give the all-time fielding cup, however, to Brian 'Groucho' Goodway, captain of the club for all too short a time before he was called away from the area to build most of the country's motorway network. 'Groucho' would patrol the majority of the off side with a strange, loping gait reminiscent of the most voluble of the Marx Brothers, hence his nickname. He caught anything which came remotely within reach, stopped everything on the ground and threw in straight over the stumps at high velocity from anywhere on even the biggest grounds. In other words he was everything you would want in a fielder. One incident stands out clearly. We had gone to South Wilts in Salisbury on a glorious Sunday in June to play against the strong Wiltshire side in which Hampset's first great County cricketer, Jim Redman, had finished his career. One of the home side's openers, a prolific left-hander, had represented Wiltshire the day before in some competition final at Lord's and had scored a ton. The stage was set for the Salisbury side to amass a large total. The first ball came from Alan Ruff, who huffed and puffed his way in and delivered what can only be described as a sighter; less charitably it might be termed a rank long-hop. The in-form batsman pulled it away disdainfully towards the distant mid-wicket boundary but 'Groucho', operating unusually on the leg-side, as the batsman was left-handed, cut it off just inside the rope. The ball was in the fielder's hand but the striker turned and announced, "Let's run the fourth, it's a long boundary." In came the throw, flat, hard and utterly accurate; the previous day's centurion was run out by a considerable margin. From hero to plonker in 24 hours, sic transit gloria; once again cricket had proved to be the great leveller. It was great to witness such exploits, though I could never replicate them. For me fielding remained something of a chore, something to be tolerated, whilst you waited to indulge in more worthwhile aspects of the game.

The most important supporting actor in the spin bowler's variety show is undoubtedly the wicketkeeper, and in this respect I have been very fortunate. A succession of extremely competent practitioners have over the years made a host of catches and stumpings beyond the call of duty. The keeper has to be in tune with what the bowler is doing, of course, and they all soon became well-versed in following the established, unchanging pattern of the six balls in my over and reacted accordingly. I think I can say that they were all schooled well before the modern era in which the wicketkeeper is expected to do more than leap around making acrobatic stops and taking any catch that flashes through off the edge. The present-day keeper has not only to do all of this but also seems to have to keep up a non-stop commentary on events. Whereas his colleagues in the slips and elsewhere in the field can, between balls and overs and in other lulls in the play, discuss at their leisure the prospects of the various mounts in the 3.30 at Kempton Park, whether they might pay a visit to The Pride of Bangladesh after the game or the particular physical attractions of mutual female acquaintances, the poor wicketkeeper has to concentrate on proclamations designed to be heard by all around him.

There appear to be many facets to this diatribe. Firstly keepers have to encourage and cajole their fielding comrades with constant eulogies couched in the most hyperbolic of terms, some of which are sadly lacking grammatically, perhaps a reflection of years of education, education, education. Thus, whenever the ball passes the bat, even if this is patently due to the total incompetence of the batsman, the modern keeper is heard to exclaim something like: "Good bowl, buddy" or if a fielder manages to make a stop well within the compass of an agile grandmother: "Great cut off, champ." The verbal diarrhoea has a more negative side to it as well in which the proverbial lowest form of wit figures highly. It is extremely important for the wicketkeeper to attempt to undermine the confidence of the batsman and to question his fitness to be out in the middle at all with gems such as: "Not good enough to get an edge to that sort of bowl" or "He didn't have a clue where that was going", the latter comment coming immediately after the ball has been dispatched off the full face of the bat to the mid-wicket boundary. Sometimes I wonder if it would be more intimidating for a batsman if he were greeted by complete silence for the duration of his time at the crease.

Even more sinister is the need to put pressure on the umpire by undermining his belief in his own ability and the suggestion that a grievous injustice just perpetrated needs to be redressed at the earliest opportunity: "Perhaps he'll hear an even thicker edge next time" after a denied caught behind or "Would have taken out all three" after a negative response to an lbw appeal. As well as feeling mental and physical fatigue after having had to concentrate on every single ball of an innings, today's wicketkeeper must surely nurse a sore jaw at the end of a day's play.

None of the Hampset keepers I played with needed to be versed in this oratorical skill; they simply got on with the job of combining with the bowler in the contest with the batsman. To the presence of mind of one of them, Keith 'Katie/KT' Tozer I am indebted for the ability to say that I took part in a genuine tie. In an early Somerset League encounter with Street we had scored 185 all out in our allotted overs and, with one ball to go, the opposition were 185 for nine. Batsman 11 faces up. Walters bowls, just short of a length and moving fractionally away. Batsman 11 misses, the ball goes through to keeper Tozer, standing back. Non-striking batsman desperately calls for a run. Non-participating fielders leap about like impotent cats on live coals. In these circumstances most keepers would almost certainly have hurled the ball at the stumps, missed and incurred overthrows but the cool Katie runs smartly to the wicket, gets within unmissable reach and calmly breaks the wicket with the batsman well out of his ground. The only complete tie I was ever involved in.

Most sojourns in the field were less dramatic, less eventful, though occasionally something of interest would occur. In a match against Taunton on the County Ground, for example, everyone was convinced that a ball from Dave Walters went straight through the stumps without disturbing anything; surely the odds on this happening must be fairly long. The most bizarre, the most farcical event, however, was at Bloomfield Rise in a match against Burnham-on-Sea. Someone bowled one of those freak balls which leaves the bowler's hand and flies off at an odd angle before coming to rest somewhere in the outfield without having passed the popping crease; in this case it was somewhere around cover point. One of our fielders wandered towards it to pick it up and return it to the bowler to see if he could actually produce a legitimate delivery. We reckoned without umpire 'Rosey', however, who in such circumstances could adopt his most formal persona full of suitable gravitas. "Fielder," he intoned, "you must leave the ball where it now lies." I was surprised he didn't say 'lieth'. Turning up the wicket he continued, "Batsman, you may play that ball if you so desire." Sensing that here was a chance to gain some cheap runs the seasider advanced towards the ball but, seeing an arc of fielders on the off-side, thought he would be clever, pirouetted on one leg and smashed the ball towards the sparsely populated on-side. Unfortunately for him, however, he succeeded only in demolishing his own stumps. This time Rosey swivelled towards the scorebox shouting, "Mr. Scorer, record the outgoing batsman as bowled," an outcome the strange delivery had hardly deserved. And the batsman wasn't even their number 11!

I don't think fielding will ever really catch on. It's a pity one cannot employ someone to represent you in the field whilst you indulge in more pleasurable activities.

Basic Skills (ii)

Batting is of course the glam side of cricket. Some would see pitting a lone fellow clad only in strategically placed light armour against a more numerous enemy as something heroic but I have always considered it a vain and arrogant activity. Moreover, a whole set of myths has been allowed to grow up around batting to maintain its exaggerated cachet. Firstly there is the overblown importance of taking guard. Batsmen try to pretend that it is a vital cog in the precision engineering of their craft. But how can standing a couple of centimetres to the left or right in the crease possibly make any difference and why, if it is so important, according to varied circumstances, does one never take off stump or middle-and-off, which would presumably be referred to as two offs? Batsmen, even those of limited skill, or perhaps even more those of limited skill, would presumably try to tell us that their judgement of the line of the ball is so fine that a correct guard is essential. In that case why ask an umpire who is 22 yards away and who may well have impaired sight, if all batsmen given out lbw are to be believed? Why can't they rely on their own judgement from a mere couple of feet? Often those wielding the bat stray from their self-imposed tethering station, only to be reined in by an admonishment from the vigilant umpire: "Batsman, you've wandered way outside leg stump." Rather than admit that they have simply lost the mark they carefully scratched in the earth not a few minutes before, most will attempt to convince all around them that this is a clever ploy, part of an intelligently worked out strategy to counter the particular bowler's plan of attack, by calling back down the wicket with perhaps even a surreptitious wink of understanding and collusion with the official, "Yes, I know, it's OK, ump, but thank you."

An even bigger con is the habit of coming to the wicket, taking guard, and then spending an interminable time looking round the field, supposedly to locate and commit to memory the exact position of all the opposing fielders. I used to make a point of moving when they had finished their panoramic searchings. These batsmen, most of whom do not have a clue about which cards have already been laid when playing rummy with their maiden aunts at Christmas or would have no idea of moves made or likely to be possible if invited to play chess, are asking us to believe that they adjust their batting according to what they have registered. They want us to think that in the split second they have to react while the ball is in mid-flight they go through all sorts of thought processes based on the memorised field of battle, deciding whether to play a particular shot or not or how to angle their bat to send the ball inches wide of the fielders. In my experience the vast majority of batsmen simply do not have this amount of brain power. What they are actually doing, I have always thought, with this charade of surveying the fielding placements is trying to see who amongst the opposition might buy them a drink in the clubhouse afterwards or whom they ought to avoid since they've been seeing rather too much of the person's wife of late. I personally have never bothered with this pretence of being able to take in all the ramifications of where the other side's fielders want to stand.

A panoramic view of the Bloomfield Rise ground about 1960. The building of new houses has not yet obscured the view northwards over the city. Many of the trees at the end of the ground were subsequently blown down in a wild storm.

In truth most of them seem to want to huddle around the bat when I'm in and there is no need to go looking for them. I have had to accept taking a guard, however, as I quickly got fed up with umpires condescendingly reminding me of the correct rites to be gone through: "Batsman, (it probably stuck in their throats to have to use such an appellation in my case) don't you want a guard?" I opted for middle and leg a) because it seemed the most popular, b) because centre was what most junior schoolboys asked for and I wanted to demonstrate that I was well past that stage and c) one leg sounded very precarious and insubstantial. So for 47 years it was "Two legs please, Mr Umpire."

Early on in my career I thought I should try to make it look as though I knew what I was doing when I came to the crease. On one particular occasion in a game against Bath at North Parade I wandered in about five to five without too much pressure on me as we had already garnered a respectable total and it was nearly time for tea, this of course was in pre-leagues days, to face Richard Andrew, who on his day could swing the ball prodigiously and who had been brought back on to mop up the tail. I took the usual two legs and then spent an exaggeratedly long time perusing the field, as I had seen those further up the order do so many times. In a puerile attempt to show everyone that this was some sort of meaningful procedure, I called down the wicket: "On second thoughts, Mr Umpire, I think I'll have one leg." I was bowled first ball. Pride before a fall. From then on I gave up on this field surveying nonsense.

It now seems to be received wisdom, promulgated mostly by TV pundits that 'everyone has to be able to bat.' Wicketkeepers must score piles of runs in the middle order or they're out, fast bowlers who have not long left the field after a gruelling spell are expected to don their pads, if necessary, and score a few runs, all bowlers

of whatever persuasion are called on to do their bit. No-one on the other hand insists that all batsmen should be available to bowl at a moment's notice. Such an attitude seeks to rid the game of one of its most endearing figures – the 'genuine number 11'. Not that long ago just about every cricket side worth its salt had one. They were instantly recognisable as they provoked an instant reaction and a flurry of activity whenever they appeared to bat. On County and even Test grounds they were accompanied to the middle by the Head Groundsman who went to the fielding side's captain to enquire of him which roller he wanted on the wicket and then hurried off to coax whatever machine had been ordered into life before the innings closed, as he confidently expected it to do imminently. At club level the emergence from the pavilion of this lone figure was always a signal for the ladies to put the kettle on and remove cling film from plates of sandwiches and cakes, if a side was batting first, or for someone to unshutter the bar and turn the gas on the beer pumps, if taking second innings.

My first experience of seeing such a character in action came when I was very small at a County game on the Rec in Bath when Somerset were entertaining high-flying Yorkshire, Fred Trueman et al. It is strange the things you remember. Of non-cricketing matters I recall only that seated next to us was a couple with a Great Dane. This huge dog sat placidly during the whole day's play and was distinguished by having pink nail varnish on its claws, perhaps an indication of some sort of canine deviance. Of the cricket all I can remember is a masterful number 11 performance from Somerset's Bryan Lobb who came in to bat when the side was in trouble and contrived to score 42, all of which were scored in areas of the ground other than that intended. The faster the fuming Tykes bowled the more our hero flashed edges in the air and along the ground but always just wide of fielders. What impressed me most was that he obviously enjoyed himself and relished the discomfiture of some inflated egos even more. This was patently behaviour to be emulated.

113

Little did I know that in years to come I would play many times against 'Lobby' when he had retired to Millfield and Morlands, Glastonbury. At those times he was always the most friendly and gentlemanly of opponents.

I am rather proud to have filled the 'genuine number 11' slot for so long at Hampset, testimony to the fact that the club's scorpion emblem does not represent a sting in the tail which, as explained before, was never the intention of the founders. I took over seamlessly from Jack Simmons, another worthy representative of the 'genuine number 11' fraternity. Jack eschewed wearing gloves and had no defensive or attacking armoury in the way of accepted shots. When the 'not playing a shot' law first came in to invalidate leg byes Jack was on one occasion sent back by an umpire intent no doubt on displaying his familiarity with the new statute. "No shot!" exclaimed the officious arbiter. "'Tis the closest I can get to one, kidder," responded Hampset's then last man. Jack performed in pre-league days and with the unfairness which affects the batting of all last men he was usually required either to go in just before tea and score as many as he could in a short time or to enter the stage as the shadows lengthened to try to secure a draw.

I am sure that Jack made a genuine attempt to do as required but his penchant for two types of beverage caused his concentration to waver when certain watersheds approached. The French refer to tea-time as *le five-o-clock,* and when this time neared on match days Jack invariably lost interest in batting in favour of partaking of his favourite brew. Equally, the opening of the bar and the consumption of a little bitter, always in half pints, had the same effect. As a young spectator I saw Jack contrive a few scratchy runs, usually off the edge, but only on one occasion did I see him make anything akin to a proper score – 48, similar in quantity and quality to Lobb's professional cameo. This innings was of such epic proportions that it drove Ernie Buck, the umpire on the day, who usually accompanied Jack to the ground on match days from their Combe Down residences, to pen a poem in its honour entitled *The day that Jack made 48*, a literary masterpiece which was published in the next edition of the Club Notes. When Jack finished playing he umpired for a while, usually for the Second Eleven. He was a good umpire and was totally unbiased, though it was strange how lbw and caught-behind appeals, against friend or foe, had a dramatically increased chance of success as five o'clock or 7.30 approached. It was a good time to bowl from Jack's end.

I had quite an act to follow in taking over the mantle of Jack Simmons but I did go one better, as far as a career best was concerned, managing to strike 49 when on tour in Wallasey. The scoreboard at one stage indicated that I had indeed reached a maiden half century so, mission accomplished and it being five o'clock or thereabouts, I duly got out, only to be told by an officious Merseyside scorer that I had been erroneously credited with a leg bye. So the top score forever remained 49.

On no other occasion did I get anywhere near the magic 50 and just about every year I took a greater number of wickets than I scored runs, a great source of satisfaction for a committed bowler. Amongst all the abject failure of ducks and golden ducks there have been the odd purple passages. I remember once hitting Colin Dredge, who was then at the height of his prowess as a County cricketer and who had come to join his myriad brothers in a league match for Frome, for a magnificent square drive for four, even if the ball did not quite travel precisely in the intended direction.

There was also the famous Chipping Sodbury cover drive, which has taken on folklore proportions. For about the only time we had gone to play the Gloucestershire side and, batting first, we did not reach a huge total against some quite hostile bowling on a sporty pitch. As usual, therefore, I went to the wicket when we were in a spot of trouble with resident number 10, Reg Trim, at the other end. I was promptly hit on the toe by a fast full toss which evoked a raucous appeal from the over-keen bowler, which was rightly turned down, and a great deal of hilarity in all but the unfortunate recipient of the blow, including my fellow batsman. Et tu Brute. After hopping around for some time I prepared to face the next ball, still smarting, both literally and metaphorically, from the recent indignity. It turned out to be a juicy half volley; for once all coordination came together and I was able to despatch the ball like lightning to the cover boundary. For years after Reg Trim opined that, from his privileged vantage point at the other end, it was the most magnificent shot he had ever seen on any ground anywhere, anytime, but he only ever said this when he was making a rather pathetic claim to take over my number 11 spot.

Perhaps my most prestigious batting entry in the scorebook might be one from a two-day County Second Eleven game at Worcestershire. It was certainly the most hopeless situation in which I have entered the fray – nine wickets down for not very many, still needing quite a few to make the opponents bat again. There were to be no Herculean efforts on this occasion; I had one ball to face from a Carter over. I played a Chinese cut and the ball went down to fine leg. In normal circumstances the better part of valour would have been not to bother to run but whoever was at the other end, either fancying a not out or himself simply preferring not to be on strike, called me for a run which it was difficult to refuse. This brought me to the other end to face the qualifying Basil d'Oliveira. Down came the ball, swinging all over the place and fizzing off the pitch, and it hit me on my static back leg. Palpably out, appeal granted. End result: Johnson lbw d'Oliveira 1. But it doesn't end there, I had been given out by Syd Buller, no less, who was at the time the most eminent umpire on the county and test circuit and who was getting back into the swing of things with an early season low-profile game on his local patch. This would definitely have been one for the scrapbook, if I'd kept one.

I can never actually remember hitting a six. I suppose by the law of averages something must have flown off the edge and over a ridiculously short boundary somewhere but I cannot recall it happening. When I suffered the indignity of having sixes hit off my bowling, I tended to think it was all rather loutish and unnecessary and so perhaps I purposely restrained myself from following suit at the crease. But I doubt if this is the real reason.

Amazingly my earliest recollection of doing anything at all meritorious on a cricket pitch involves batting rather than bowling. In one of my first Second Eleven games we went to Stoke Bishop in Bristol. The home side got plenty and we made a less than impressive reply with the end result that I made my way to the wicket at ten past seven with an impossible target and one wicket left and joined a similarly youthful Sam Shearn. There was still the draw to play for in these innocent pre-league days but hardly anyone seemed to think this a realistic prospect as everyone on our side disappeared to shower, change, pack their bags and stow them in cars.

The opposition fielders gathered closely around the two hapless 14-year-olds, no doubt relishing the prospect of victory and an early opportunity to quench their thirst in the bar. I tried not to back away even without the sharpened stump behind ready to impale me. I tried also to recall all that Ken Saunders and company had drummed into us, head straight and still, elbow up, bat and pad together, bat dead straight and angled down. I doubt if we scored many runs but somehow we held out much to the annoyance of the increasingly tetchy opposition bowlers and fielders. We came off having secured an inglorious draw and having kept our hosts out of the bar until the regulation time, which was more helpful to their livers long term but not for their temperament at the time.

Simon 'Sam' Shearn and myself at about the age we mounted our heroic rearguard action. Master Shearn seems to be contemplating something equally mischievous. To our right is Jimmy Wood, a representative for Whitbread's who ensured the club was stocked with Trophy Bitter and other essential supplies. Shortly after this Jimmy came to an untimely end in mysterious circumstances whilst on holiday in Greece.

Arguably my greatest triumph with the bat came, however, at the other end of my career when I won a game single-handedly (well, almost) without even putting bat to ball. There is nothing a genuine number 11 likes better, apart from being left in peace to do the crossword and not having to bat at all, than going to the wicket and having the person at the other end get out before he can face a ball. Second to this comes being run out without facing a ball, for there is always someone else to blame. If you do have to go to the wicket it is certainly best to do so if the person just out has been dismissed on the last ball of an over. This at least allows a bit of a breathing space.

This highly desired scenario came about in a tense Second Eleven encounter at Timsbury. The Home side made 192, and when I was called on to appear we had just lost our ninth man to the last ball of the penultimate over and were 184 for nine, six balls to go, one wicket left, nine runs required for victory. Our score had been largely due to a resolute innings from Colin Sinkins who had been in most of the innings and was about 80 not out. This had been a typical Sinkins knock, full of deft nudges and glances, quick running and finely judged shots but certainly nothing desperately agricultural. Timsbury were fielding an out-of-form First Eleven bowler intent on regaining his senior place and it was he who had inflicted most of the damage and was of course due to bowl the last over. I strolled to the middle perfectly happy that I did not have to face and was greeted by the well ensconced Sinkins. "We can still do this, Blocker," he opined in up-beat mode and added by way of strategy, "I'll do the calling, run hard and try to give me the bowling." I looked at him in amazement. "You don't think I'm going down that ******** end, do you?" I retorted, the question being entirely rhetorical. To back up my contribution to the tactical conversation I turned on my heel and went to my end where, taking off my gloves, I sat on my bat, a stance designed entirely to convince my fellow batsman that any remote chance of victory was entirely in his court. To demonstrate his credentials as a proper batsman Colin did the looking around the field bit. I, of course, realised that was merely to give himself thinking time, but everyone else probably thought that there was some point to it.

The first ball is delivered, just short of a length on off stump. Leaning back, our last hope plays a delicate late cut that sends the ball safely along the ground, just evading third man for four. Five required off five sounds more promising. The next ball is a beauty which is only just kept out. More definite contact is made with the third; in other circumstances a scampered single might have been contemplated but my lack of interest in such heroics is still more than apparent. Things are getting more tense.

It was then that something entirely out of character and unexpected happened. A similar ball is delivered but the mainstay of our innings, who has thus far displayed a complete lack of any flamboyance, now decides that desperate measures are required and advances a few steps down the wicket, depositing the ball well into the Timsbury tennis courts way beyond the mid-wicket boundary. Victory by one wicket with two balls to spare. I feel I am completely justified in leading everyone off the pitch, acknowledging the admiring applause. If it had not been for my resolute refusal to contemplate going to the hot seat of the striker's end we would never have achieved such an exciting win.

There were never any serious contenders for my number 11 slot. Most people actually seem to want to bat and so to have a genuine number 11 in the side is useful for a captain since he does not have to ask anyone else to bat in a position which they presumably find infra dig. Reg Trim tried to suggest sometimes that he, as number 10, swap with me, since he was 'seriously out of form'. When I pointed out that I had never been in such a state as 'in form', the matter was settled. As I grew older and even less proficient with the bat I played more and more often with Bill Day who did provide genuine contention for the coveted position. B Day or 'Bidet', as he was very appropriately known, since his batting was very much like the English attitude to that rather peculiar continental piece of sanitary ware in that everyone thought it should come in handy but no-one quite knew what to do with it, just did not seem able to take the overrated activity of batting seriously. Opposition bowlers never quite fathomed what to make of 'Bidet', since each ball, whether it dismissed him or not, was greeted with gales of laughter by the, for want of a better term, batsman. No-one knew if this hilarity was caused by his own inability to make contact or by his amused contempt for the delivery he had just faced. It got to such a pitch at one stage that whenever Bill and I featured in the same side we were simply instructed to 'sort out 10 and 11 yourselves.'

When I eventually dropped down from the First Eleven, Andy O'Donnell tended to take over as last man but he was never a genuine number 11, as he could certainly bat. This is proved by the many magnificent shots he has been seen to make and by a faded newspaper cutting he once showed us in which he featured as a long-haired youth resembling Jethro Tull who had impressively won the Blackpool and District single-wicket competition. A genuine number 11 would not even aspire to enter such a challenge.

Billy Hallett is the next longest-serving number 11 but we did not often play in the same side and so there was rarely any wrangling between us for the last position in the batting order. Often on tour of course we did appear in the team together and there was obviously little to separate us in terms of incompetence. In one match at Liss in Hampshire we came together at the crease at about a quarter to five with a reasonable score on the board but probably not enough to bowl at if one of us got out immediately. I do not believe in lengthy conferences between an incoming batsman and the colleague who is already in, it just seems to delay the inevitable, but on this occasion I thought I had better relay some instructions to Bill. "They say it doesn't really matter if we don't score any more runs," I told Bill, "but apparently we should stay in until five o'clock." " Righto, Blocker," acquiesced Bill. The home side's opening bowler had been brought back to polish off the tail and duly produced a very respectable delivery, but, to everyone's amazement, it was sent straight back over the bowler's head into the car park of the Spread Eagle public house. I felt this was entirely inappropriate behaviour and so, considering myself for once the senior partner, I advanced down the wicket and upbraided my hot-headed colleague, ordering him to 'calm down and bat properly'. He had the good grace to apologise, muttering something about a rush of blood to the head. But his contrition did not last long for he tried to send the second delivery out of the ground in precisely the same direction. This time, however, he got the elevation slightly wrong and the ball spiralled skywards almost vertically and came down to the bowler who promptly dropped it. In all the confusion, however, we had both ended up in the same crease and one of us was run out. This is the pure farce which is bound to be caused by having two genuine number 11s at the wicket together.

Helmets for batsmen have been a great innovation, particularly at first class level, where they have no doubt prevented some very serious injuries. Even in a modest club context they are a good idea and I do not subscribe to the idea that to make young people wear them amounts to some sort of mollycoddling. For at least half of my career, however, they were unknown, and I myself have only ever worn a 'lid' once – for one ball. This was against Bristol West Indians in a game in which we were severely thrashed. The match took place in Bristol, the home side amassed a large total and when we came to reply we were immediately faced with two very quick bowlers out to finish the game off as quickly as possible. On seeing the first couple of overs I immersed myself in the crossword, hoping above hope that the others would be able to withstand the onslaught and that I would not be required. For a while all went well and we progressed to about 90 for one, thanks largely to one of the bravest innings I have ever seen from a Hampset batsman by Paul Collard. Helmetless, he withstood a fearful battering, taking many blows on the upper body and even the head. Finally a slight miscue flew off the top edge and he was caught at third man. The rest of the side capitulated and we succumbed to about 125 for nine. I felt for the first time ever that a helmet might be a useful piece of equipment, borrowed one of the two or three that the whole side possessed, strapped it on and, not seeing very well, tried to find my way to the wicket like some medieval knight taking part in an annual jousting competition. The West Indian bowler came pounding over the horizon and bore down on me intent on delivering an exocet type missile. Mercifully he pitched it up and I groped forward with what I thought was an immaculate Ken-Saunders-taught forward defensive stroke, short backlift, eyes horizontal and focussed, bat and pad together, left elbow up.

Unfortunately I played this textbook shot two seconds after the ball had sent the middle stump cartwheeling out of the ground much to the raucous delight of the fielders and, more embarrassingly, to that of the considerable number of West Indian spectators around the ground. The whole sorry scene would have made an excellent advert in that series where they tell you that you should have gone to a well known High Street chain of providers of spectacles. With fairly undisguised relief I rushed off still wearing the helmet but with impaired vision I went straight into the opposition dressing room by mistake. "Sorry, man, we don't need you, we got plenty of rabbits of our own here, dey makin' holes all over de outfield," cried one of the victorious West Indian as they came in after me but then, generously thrusting a can of Red Stripe in my hand, tempered the blow with "Try dis man, 'tis tastier dan lettuce leaves."

My most embarrassing 'first-baller', however, occurred much earlier in my career and was due entirely to a piece of eccentricity on the part of the then captain of the Second Eleven, Bernard King. We travelled to Devizes on a Sunday when it had rained most of the morning but had turned out beautifully sunny in the afternoon. Bernard won the toss and sensibly elected to field and our seamers, Cyril Butler to the fore, soon had the home side in all sorts of trouble and they were dismissed for a bit less than 100 by 4.30. Tea was not ready and we were asked to start our innings before the interval. Soon we were about 25 for three, one of the dismissed being our skipper after one of his typical cameo innings – ..66w. At about 4.50 I was suddenly asked to go in to act as 'tea watchman', surely an invention of our captain thinking outside the box! The ploy did not work. I was out first ball and the ignominy did not end there; I got out in about the most inappropriate way imaginable in the situation – stumped! It must have been about this time that it dawned on people that I had neither the ability nor the temperament to become a batsman and I was allowed to become a genuine number 11 of whom nothing was expected.

When you get dismissed so quickly, so often, you tend to get quite good at inventing excuses. Lbw is about the best way for an ineffectual number 11 to go since, in your defence, you can always invoke a certain element of doubt. First of all you can claim you hit it but with such a fine edge that the snick was audible only to an alert dog, the sound not being within the auditory range of the average umpire or any other human being. Otherwise, as long as you get reasonably well forward, you can argue that the ball moved so much off the pitch that the laws of geometry, presumably unknown to the mathematically challenged umpire, should have precluded the appeal being given. Most of these pretences are spurious but I am sure that many number 11s are given out either simply to put them out of their misery like some stricken animal or because there is little point in prolonging the inevitable. This is hard to justify as long as euthanasia remains illegal in this country.

I am sure a mercy killing of this sort happened one day when we were playing Taunton. This was one of the very first games played on Taunton's new ground once they had left the County Ground. An early indication that that we had a rather officious neutral umpire to contend with came when he claimed that he could not see the boundary rope from the middle and demanded that the home captain have pieces of toilet paper tied around the rope at regular intervals to make the line more visible. We bowled Taunton out for a gettable total but then got into trouble ourselves, largely because of the bowling of Dennis Breakwell, who at the time was still a successful county cricketer. When I went in there was little chance of avoiding defeat, even though an established batsman, I think it was Pete Mines, was still in at the other end. I had one ball from Breakwell to survive. I went so far forward I was nearer the bowler than the wicketkeeper before being hit on the pad. The ball moved appreciably off the wicket and, even if it hadn't, I am sure there was no way anyone could say with certainty that it was going to hit the stumps. Geometrical implausibility did not seem to count with this umpire, however, he upheld a half-hearted appeal from the bowler and sent me packing to the pavilion – game over. As we trooped off I enquired whether we should collect up the bits of toilet paper which still festooned the boundary rope in case he had any more crap to dispense but this did not go down too well.

After lbw the next best way to be out is to be caught behind off the thinnest of edges. You can always claim that you did not hit the ball and of course there are lots of ways to explain away the definite sound heard by everyone on the ground. These include "I hit my pad on the way through", "it must have been the bat hitting the ground" and "the ball brushed my thigh". The very best thing to do, but something which must not be overdone, is to inspect the off stump and marvel at the fact that the ball, which had definitely clipped it, as it went past, had miraculously not dislodged a bail. It tests the ingenuity of a number 11 to explain away a dismissal when you have lost your middle stump or have ballooned a dolly catch to mid-off or short extra cover. Vociferous attempts at justification such as "I wasn't ready" or "I'm sure that was a no-ball" wear a little thin after a while.

All in all, batting was definitely a pastime to be avoided. My favourite scorebook entry remained D.N.B., the genuine number 11's equivalent of R.I.P.

Basic Skills (iii)

Bowling is, of course, the supreme art of cricket. It is in this ever changing, ever developing skill that individual expertise is allied with collective participation to bring about the desired result, the dismissal of the common enemy, the batsman. The bowler, the officer in the field, perhaps in consultation with his commander-in-chief, plots the downfall of the foe, occasionally brings it about on his own but is more likely to call up reinforcements from the ranks of the foot-soldiering fielders and sends the enemy scurrying back to his quarters – preferably without having registered any record of his presence. I missed out, thank goodness, on National Service by several years, perhaps bowling was one way of getting combat experience.

One great thing about this noble art is that, even after a set-back, perhaps after having been unceremoniously slogged out of the ground over mid-wicket from a loose delivery, the bowler can compose himself and take the fight to the batsman again, whereas the latter, quite rightly, has one chance, unless of course it's a no-ball. If you're really brave, after such a setback, you can even tempt the slogger to do the same again and hope that a slight variation on your part and over-weaning pride on his might combine to send him contritely back to the pavilion. Spin-bowling, once thought to be a dying trade, is, moreover, the finest manifestation of the art for one's weaponry consists of subtlety and guile, rather than sheer power.

Satisfaction can be gained in ways other than just taking a great number of wickets, pleasurable as that might be. For example, it is almost as rewarding to bowl an economical spell which prevents a good opposition from reaching the required total for victory as it is to dismiss a less talented side for a paltry score. The quality of the pitch can also come into play. To bowl a side out on a wicket 'turning square' is almost like an unpleasant duty which has to be done, whereas to take a few wickets for not too many on a batsman's paradise is more heart-warming.

A bowler's performance also quite often depends on what is going on at the other end. I do not have any statistics to back up the impression, but I am fairly certain that the large number of overs I sent down were delivered with a relatively small number of co-plotters operating from the other end. The fact that Dave Walters, John Bissex, Reg Trim, Sam Shearn, Andy O'Donnell and John Flagg were such good, accurate practitioners who were usually getting wickets and tying the batsmen down caused many impatient opponents to have a go with injudicious shots at what I could float up from my end.

Conditions and circumstances also play a great part. Cricket is not meant to be conducted in anything other than completely dry conditions. If even the slightest drizzle came down I was all for calling the whole thing off, as the song goes, for a master practitioner cannot be expected to ply his trade with a damp ball. In such circumstances one can try to influence the umpire into going off in a variety of ways. Turning up one's collar and looking thoroughly miserable is a first step, expressing the wish that the umpire will not catch his death of cold is another, as is purposely slipping prior to delivering the ball and calling for copious supplies of sawdust. Incidentally where do clubs get sawdust from these days? We used to go to the local butcher, but his supply tended to be laced with blood, gore and gristle.

Less subtle ways of trying to convince umpires of the need to leave the playing area are making claims that it is raining much harder in the outfield than in the middle or sheltering under an umbrella at third man. The most difficult situation arises when you are in the middle of a violent thunderstorm but it is not actually raining. We once played against Shirehampton at Bloomfield Rise when I swear the lightning was dancing off the stumps but no precipitation was falling. In the end the batsman persuaded the umpire he couldn't concentrate and we all fled. Soon after it bucketed down, which justified our withdrawal.

The presence of left-handed batsmen is discomforting for the average bowler. Somewhere in the depths of Somerset we played in a match in which the other side fielded no less than nine such unnatural specimens, a most unsportsmanlike thing to do. I cannot remember exactly where this was but it must have occurred in some remote backwater where in-breeding was rife.

In theory the arm ball, moving away from left-handers, should have been productive against these cack-handers but I could rarely seem to get it in the right place. Received wisdom suggested that it was better to bowl around the wicket to these people but I preferred still to appear from behind the umpire. However, round the wicket, I tried to get as close to the official as possible to facilitate a slightly different line. Sometimes this slight shift in approach resulted in giving the umpire a thwack around the ear in the follow-through which did not exactly endear one to the adjudicator and led, I am sure, to some legitimate appeals against left-handers being rejected out of pique.

Johnson's 100th wicket

Hampset slow left arm bowler, Malcolm Johnson, captured his 100th wicket of the season for weekend matches in the game with Midsomer Norton.

It is the first time a Hampset cricketer has achieved this milestone for 26 years. The last player to do it was Jim Redman way back in 1952.

Malcolm, who was born in Bath, is now a school-teacher in the Southampton area but commutes every weekend to turn out for his local club in the Somerset League.

The batsman at the non-striking end when I accomplished this feat was Ian McDonald, a leg-spinner who approached the wicket with a limping run, the result, I believe, of an accident when young and who, year after year took a sackful of wickets for Midsomer Norton. Hearing that the applause was louder and more prolonged than usual he asked the reason. He seemed underwhelmed by the explanation. I realised afterwards that this was not caused by pique or resentment, for 'Mac' was the most engaging of opponents. It was simply because he did something similar every year.

Unfortunately not all squares are completely flat; after all, Lord's is reputed to have quite a pronounced slope. The elevation of such inclines is even more marked in some modest clubs. The presence of such a slope always made the choice of ends a little problematic. All in all, I think I think I preferred to try to turn the ball up a hill for the batsman could not then play with the spin and simply send the ball hurtling down the incline through the offside. Until you got to know away venues well, the question from the skipper, "Which end do you prefer here?", was not as easy as it sounded. Up the slope, if there was one, and with the shorter boundary on the leg-side, to encourage hitting against the spin, was a good starting point. When all things were equal it was best simply to choose the end which gave you quickest access to the more pleasant of the two possible third man positions to which you could repair at the end of each over. At Bloomfield Rise this of course meant the Pavilion end. All the fielders after a bit knew where to go, they just trooped off undirected to their fielding stations in the same way a herd of bloated cows knows its way to the milking parlour at the appropriate time. Of the 10,508.3 overs I apparently sent down (don't forget the .3) only a handful were from the 'big house' end. Performances in this unfamiliar territory left much to be desired, I just did not seem able to orientate myself properly and innovative captains who thought they might try something different by asking me to operate from the wrong end soon gave up their experiments and reverted to the status quo. At away venues, or even at home, if anything untoward happened, there was the rather tedious business of setting the field. I tended to let the captain get on with it, after all that's what he was there for, and I was too busy contemplating the delivery of the next ball.

With a short, seven paces arching run I tended to come in on quite flat, level terrain. For some bowlers with longer run-ups the ground was sometimes more difficult. When Burnham-on-Sea moved temporarily to a small prep school ground, while their new headquarters were being prepared, Bob Clapp came in from a cabbage patch in an adjacent allotment and through an open garden gate. At a ground we visited on tour in the New Forest the square was on a sort of plateau high above the undulating outfield. Opening bowlers with approaches of even modest length were at first invisible to the batsmen and close fielders and appeared over the horizon rather unexpectedly at times, like the cavalry in the B movies we delighted in at Saturday morning pictures. It was about the only occasion when the rather pathetic claim that "I wasn't ready" from a dismissed batsman was almost legitimate. The most difficult conditions for bowlers of all types are when a pronounced slope goes along the same line as the wicket, rather then across it. This was the case at a ground on a cliff somewhere just over the border in North Devon where we were once called upon to perform. Alan Ruff took the first over down the slope. In the best of circumstances Ruffy's first ball was often as wayward as his unruly, leonine hair and in this case he just kept running when he reached the wicket somehow unable to release the ball as his high stepping legs whirred beneath him. It was not much better from the other end either as a succession of bowlers tried to operate up a steep hill into a howling gale straight off the ocean. With local knowledge the home side mastered the conditions with no fuss at all but from all our bowlers there was much wailing and gnashing of teeth, the sound of which was borne inland on the prevailing winds.

It is always a good idea to get the umpire well disposed to you. Just as Sgt. Wilson in *Dad's Army* was always soft-soaping the ladies, a little bit of ingratiating never goes amiss for a bowler. At the beginning of a spell, therefore, it was cap off, folded and handed with deference to the official to whom it was politely announced, "Left-arm round please", adding "Would you mind standing up to the wicket, please?" On a cold day an umpire is probably quite happy to be handed a sweater but otherwise it is as well to be slightly apologetic: " Sorry to burden you with this, Mr. Umpire, but would you mind awfully taking this sweater?" The most officious – and deaf – umpire I ever encountered was from Stapleton. He failed to hear the 'Left-arm round please' bit and, when I delivered the first ball, he no-balled me for 'not announcing the mode of delivery'. "But I did," I retorted. "I even said please, you prick." The last two words were said *sotto voce* as I turned away so that he could not hear them. The Stapleton batsman grudgingly confirmed that the proper procedures had been gone through, but I was still incensed and I proceeded to take nine wickets. A pity I didn't come across hard-of-hearing umpires more often.

I went one better than nine on just one occasion but even this failed to alter the stereotyped after-match conversation with my mother who had a series of set phrases which she always used in particular situations. For instance, when planning anything in the future, such as Christmas and other fixed holidays, she prefaced all her remarks with the gloomy caveat, "If we are spared …." After all public holidays of whatever length which brought about the closure of shops on normal opening days she forever pronounced herself to be "all out with the days". On Christmas Day the merest glimpse of a ray of sunshine was greeted with the claim that "the sun always shines on Christmas Day", which I suppose is true, if you think about it, but the claim that it shone on Odd Down was less easy to uphold. If, in the run-up to Christmas, anyone told her that the shops were not absolutely heaving with people, this was greeted in boom or bust alike with the knowing assertion that "there's not the money about." Thus she always asked how a cricket match had gone, when I returned home for the night in my younger days or to fetch my car in later ones, with a fixed set of phrases with a few variables depending on the answers she received. The conversation every time went like this:

Mother: "How did you get on?"

MJ: "We won/lost/drew/tied." (This last alternative could only be used properly on one occasion.)

M: "Did you take any wickets?"

MJ: "Any number from 0 to 10" or " I didn't get on today".

M: "Oh, that's good" or "I don't expect it was your wicket." (This commendable acceptance that failure to dismiss anyone was entirely to be explained by adverse playing conditions, even if it was rather oddly expressed, was very prescient). "Did you get any runs?"

MJ: "Any number from 0 to about 10 – rarely more" or " No, I didn't have to go in."

M: "Well, you did your bit." (This, even if I had just announced that I had neither batted nor bowled. It was stretching even a mother's bias to suggest I had 'done my bit' with my fielding). "Would you like a nice cup of tea?"

MJ: "No thanks, I'll be peeing all night." (Forecast of such incontinent behaviour had nothing to do with the diuretic properties of the national beverage but was based more on the quantity of Whitbread Trophy Bitter consumed – though not in my car-driving days, I hasten to add) or " No, I'd better get on" (if I was driving home).

M: "No, I don't think I will either, I don't want to be getting out in the night."

The attempt to avoid disturbed nights, which became harder in direct proportion to the weakening of the bladder, formed part of her conviction that a good night's sleep was all-important and always led her to enquire first thing in the morning, of family members and occasional guests alike, if one had slept well. Fortunately with the latter she did not extend her concerned enquiries to cover the state of the bowels. Towards the end of her innings she became partial to a small glass of Benedictine in the evening because "it helps me sleep and doesn't seem to get me out in the night." I was once told on a trip around the Benedictine distillery in Fécamp that it had secret ingredients and properties, a bit like Coca-Cola, but I'm not sure that this quality of avoiding nocturnal urination was quite what the Normandy monks had in mind.

August 14th 1983 was quite a significant date, for it was on that day that I managed to take all ten of Shirehampton's wickets. Against a strong Bristol side it was just one of those days when everything went right. There were plenty of others when the complete opposite was true. The ball did not turn viciously; it mostly deviated about half the width of the bat and moved quite quickly. Every catch stuck from my end and the other bowlers had all the bad luck going. I think the one most to suffer was Reg Trim, but serves him right since the scorecard reveals that he had somehow commandeered my rightful batting position. I note that I batted at no. 10 (6 not out, no less) and R.Trim D.N.B. I cannot recall why this upheaval in the customary batting order took place on that day. All I can think is that an unsuspecting captain, Pete Thomas, was persuaded by constant references to the Chipping Sodbury cover drive to upset the natural order of things. Nor can I remember the exact details of any of the wickets to fall that day except for the last one. As usual I relied heavily on back-up from the fielders for the record shows that eight of the opposition batsmen were caught and two were stumped. As far as the final dismissal is concerned, all ten must have been seen as a possibility for unusually a gully was put in and Shirehampton's no. 10 duly obliged by directing a low catch into Adrian Jeffrey's reliable hands.

HAMPSET v SHIREHAMPTON

Bloomfield Rise, 14 August 1983

Hampset won by 72 runs

HAMPSET

Batsman	Fielder	Bowler	Runs
E. Burns		b Forde (R)	14
C. Sinkins	c Geddes	b Carter	32
R. Holmes	c Lewis (R)	b Carter	10
D. Hayward	c Osborne	b Forde (M)	13
P. Mines	c Osborne	b Forde (M)	59
P. Thomas		b Forde (M)	26
A. Jeffrey	c Read	b Forde (M)	2
C. Hack	run out		0
N. Guy	c Carter	b Forde (M)	11
M. Johnson	not out		6
R. Trim	did not bat		
	Extras		32
	(for 9 wickets)		**205**

SHIREHAMPTON

Batsman	Fielder	Bowler	Runs
M. Bowyer	c Guy	b Johnson	28
C. Read	st Thomas	b Johnson	0
I. Osborne	c Jeffrey	b Johnson	0
K. Earl	c Hayward	b Johnson	0
D. Woolley	c and	b Johnson	25
I. Lewis	c Trim	b Johnson	15
A. Geddes	c Sinkins	b Johnson	34
M. Forde	st Thomas	b Johnson	1
A. Carter	c Sinkins	b Johnson	14
R. Forde	c Jeffrey	b Johnson	11
R. Lewis	not out		4
	Extras		1
			133

M. Johnson 20.1-3-53-10

"Well, you did your bit then."

After this abnormal occurrence and not a little celebration afterwards, (my relatively newly acquired wife was proving quite useful as a driver after matches), the post-match debriefing with my mother went completely along familiar lines:

Mother: "How did you get on?"

MJ : "We won by 72 runs."

M: "Did you take any wickets?"

MJ (excitedly): "I got all ten."

M: "Oh, that's good. Did you make any runs?"

MJ: "Yes, 6 not out."

M: "Well, you did your bit then. Would you like a nice cup of tea?"

MJ: "No, I think we'd better be getting back."

Not surprisingly it was not possible to emulate that heady performance of August 14th 1983, but I kept trying for over 20 years and managed to persuade a number of batsmen that it was time to return to the comforts of the pavilion. The great thing about bowling is that you have constantly to adapt; you are learning all the time. It is certainly true that right to the end the challenge was always different, demanding a varied approach, although only with slight variations on the theme of my core repertoire of six balls. In my very last match, for example, a league game against Timsbury Second Eleven from which we emerged as victors, I definitely learnt something new: that, when you are playing against a side half of whose members have been out the previous night on the captain's stag do, it is essential merely to bowl straight. I managed to do this and succeeded in bowling a couple of the hung-over carousers.

I think I've already nominated eight records for my desert island, but I'm going to crave one more. As the last record, therefore, I should like something utterly cheesy and unimaginative, Frank Sinatra's version of Paul Anka's *My Way*. They were both obviously thinking of how to bowl the ideal over when they wrote/sang it. I can tell them how it's done – three orthodox slow left arm deliveries, the Bishen Bedi Bawdrip ball, one angled in to the batsman from wide of the crease and then the arm ball to round it off. Try it sometime.

Poppy, a thoroughbred 'Life of Reilly' cat
with the rest of the Johnson family in 2010.